Developing Christian Education in the smaller Church

Developing Christian Education in the smaller Church

CAROLYN C. BROWN

A Griggs Educational Resource

Published by
ABINGDON PRESS / NASHVILLE

DEVELOPING CHRISTIAN EDUCATION IN THE SMALLER CHURCH

Fifth Printing 1990

Library of Congress Cataloging in Publication Data

BROWN, CAROLYN C. (Carolyn Carter), 1947-
Developing Christian education in the smaller church.
(A Griggs educational resource)
1. Christian education. 2. Small churches. I. Title.
BV1471.2.B73 268 81-17563 AACR2

ISBN 0-687-10508-0

Dedicated to all people who are committed to building effective ministries of Christian education in their own small churches.

MANUFACTURED IN THE UNITED STATES OF AMERICA

Contents

Introduction: How to Use This Book

This book grows out of four years' work as Director of Christian Education in a cluster of seven small churches in Orange County, North Carolina. They ranged in size from thirty-seven to one hundred sixty members. Some were clearly rural churches. One was a small town church set in the middle of a historical district. Another was a rural church becoming a suburban church as a nearby city was growing out to include it. In one of the smallest, there were nearly no children in the congregation. Another was made up almost entirely of members of one family. Some supported their own full-time minister, and some shared their minister with another church. In short, the cluster included nearly a complete cross-section of small-church situations.

When I arrived, I was fairly confident that I knew what to do to serve these churches and how I would go about doing it. I had served one church of three hundred twenty members and another of twelve hundred. Though there had been some differences in what was needed and how one worked to meet those needs in those churches, the similarities were more obvious than the differences. So, I figured that the same basic approaches that had worked in the others would work in these smaller churches.

It was not too long before I realized that I was wrong. The systems of committees, long-range planning by objectives, and class arranging just did not fit at all. Things were done much more informally. In the smallest churches, there was more work to be done than people to staff separate committees to oversee each task. Decisions and plans were made by whoever was working on or interested in some project. In one church, the adult Sunday school class did the usual work of a Christian Education committee. Grouping people for Sunday school classes required freedom to ignore every pattern suggested by the denomination in order to respond to the numbers, ages, and interests of these particular students. Once classes were arranged, there was often no curriculum that really fit us, because all curricula are planned for graded classes with no more than two or three grades in a class. We often had four to six grades in a class.

I also learned that almost every small church includes a group of people who care passionately about Christian education and work long past the call of duty to see that the youth are nurtured, the Sunday school is alive and interesting, and church members are offered chances to keep growing spiritually. Together, these groups of caring people and I went to work building the kinds of opportunities for Christian growth we wanted. Slowly, we began to learn some methods and to develop some ideas that worked. It has been a piecemeal kind of learning. One idea worked, so we would try to remember it. Another method failed, so we would try to figure out why and then forget the failure. The process continues. We have developed no one system that is THE ANSWER to education in all small churches. What we have learned is some workable ways to go about tackling some typical small-church education tasks.

This book is a collection of those "ways to do the job." It is not a theory book, but a workbook. Therefore, it is not meant to be read and then saved on a shelf, but to be written in and even cut up by people as they go about doing the educational work of the church. Many chapters offer step-by-step directions on how to do a particular educational task. There are several ways you could use this book. Three are listed below, but there are others, I am sure. Think of who does the education work in your church and how they do it. That plus the three possibilities listed here, should give you some ideas of how to use the book in your church.

(1) It would be possible to use the different chapters as the need arises. For example, if you have an opening assembly, it may run smoothly and meaningfully for years, needing minimum attention. Then, rumblings erupt. One group considers it a waste of time, or wants to change it, or just stops coming to it, while another group cannot imagine Sunday school without it and considers the opposition to be near-heretics. The chapter on "Those @#*#@ Opening Assemblies" may not be appropriate until the rumblings arise. At that point, it may offer a way to resolve the conflict.

(2) On the other hand, if you have a group that meets regularly to plan for the educational life of your church, that group might want to earmark the chapter appropriate to the agenda of each meeting for the year. Committee members could agree to read that chapter before the meeting. Some of the processes in the chapters could become the method by which the committee does its work during the meeting.

(3) Finally, if your church has no committee charged with overseeing the educational life of the church, a group of people interested and active in education at your church could work through the book together and make suggestions to the proper people and/or official boards. If you do this, it would be wise to clear your plan with your ruling board FIRST, so that your suggestions are listened to as more than the work of a bunch of busybodies.

One warning: This book is best worked through with at last one other person and preferably a group of people. There are two reasons for this. (1) It requires that you objectively evaluate a church you care about. Several caring heads will usually produce clearer objectivity than one, because our caring tends to produce blind spots. (2) It is frustrating to be the only person with a vision. If several people share in creating a vision, they can support each other as, together, they try to pass it on to others and implement it. So share the work and the satisfaction.

Part One:
Who Is Responsible for Education in a Small Church?

Christian education does not just happen. Let me rephrase that. GOOD Christian education does not just happen. But you would be surprised by how many church schools in small churches seem to just happen. Pretty much the same teachers keep teaching the same curriculum, in the same way, in the same room, to the same orderly procession of students. Questions like who plans for the church school, and who is responsible for what goes on, get blank quizzical stares for answers. "No one, really, I guess. It just sort of happens." Most of these church schools tend to be rather ho-hum places. That is why the starting point for building a good church school is to identify some group as being *responsible* for making GOOD Christian education happen in their church.

Most denominations suggest who these responsible people should be and how they should be organized to carry out these responsibilities. Most often, the suggestion is that a committee be formed to oversee all the education work of a church. It may be called the Education Committee, the Christian Education Committee, the Strengthening the Church Committee, the Nurture Committee, or anything else, but its task is the same. The committee is to meet regularly (usually monthly) to administer ongoing programs, plan special events, and respond to new educational needs and ideas as they arise. Often it is suggested that there needs to be a subcommittee doing the detail work on each ongoing ministry. For example, there might be a Sunday School Committee, a Youth Work Committee, etc. The committee and each subcommittee should include a few leaders involved in that ministry and a few members at large.

There are many advantages to this organization. For one thing, there is a group that meets *regularly* for the sole purpose of directing the church's educational ministry. That should mean that a group is doing deliberate planning and evaluating of programs, rather than just pumping out "what has always been done." So, instead of the church school superintendent just reordering the study series used last year, a committee can ask whether that series is what is needed for the coming year. Or, as Christmas approaches, a committee can explore how we can best grow in our faith through the church's educational celebrations of the season. But if some group does not schedule the time for this kind of evaluation and planning, it will most likely not get done, and educational ministry will lack the thoughtful direction it needs. A committee that meets regularly provides time for such discussions.

If a committee is meeting regularly to oversee all of a church's educational work, there will also be coordination that is otherwise lacking. On the most basic level, the communication provided by this committee should insure that education events are not in conflict with each other. For example, it should reduce the chances that the youth fellowship will be on a retreat and miss the Rally Day program that the church school superintendent planned to be especially appealing to youth, as happened in one small church. A committee can keep everyone aware of what is going on in other parts of the educational ministry. This awareness can lead to coordination on deeper levels. For example, the committee could direct the different activities youth are involved in so that they complement, rather than contradict or mimic, each other. If church school class is to be primarily Bible study, and there is a softball team on which all the youth play, the fellowship group may need to concentrate on mission projects and studying youth issues. Thus all the needs of youth are responded to. The church's educational ministry is more well-rounded as a result of this coordination.

A committee that meets regularly can, furthermore, catch potential problems and resolve them before they become major crises. For one thing, there is a group to which people can go with a gripe or an idea about something better. The parent who is unhappy that his child is not learning the catechism, the adult who is about to quit coming to Sunday school rather than face the boring teacher again, and the young people who want to go on a retreat like their friends' church did, all have someone to approach for a hearing. Without this group to take their request to, their only hope is to agitate for help among their friends. Such agitation usually causes some unfortunate and unintended dissension and conflict. A committee that meets regularly provides a forum that makes such conflict avoidable. An alert committee can even spot potential problems before someone raises them. All of this produces a more smoothly running educational ministry.

There is not a church of any size that would not benefit from the overseeing and direction such a committee provides. The committee, however, need not be exactly what the denominational patterns suggest. For one thing, most small churches do not need all those suggested subcommittees. While a church that sponsors a junior high fellowship, a senior high fellowship, a series of sports teams, yearly communicants' classes, and five youth church-school classes would surely need a youth subcommittee to plan and coordinate all their work, a church with fewer than ten teen-agers, who are included in one church school class and meet for fellowship Sunday evening, would be adequately covered if one of their advisors or a mature teen-ager served on the education committee. Furthermore, many education committees do not need all the suggested members. In a church of one hundred or less, a committee of nine is an overload. Four or five key people can probably do the job, if they represent all the educational work of that church and are in touch with all groups within the congregation. It is a matter of common sense. We need enough of an organization to support our ministry, but not so much that there are no people with time and energy to do the ministry.

The job of regular overseeing does not even have to be done by a "committee." In one church of less than fifty members, the adult Sunday school class serves all the functions of this committee. They select the curriculum, discuss new possibilities, identify and deal with problems, and recruit teachers. Two or three Sunday morning sessions a year are fully devoted to this work. Further work is done in five minutes before or after class, as the need arises. Everyone in the church knows that if you have an idea or complaint, it goes to that class. For that church it is a quite workable way to provide regular supervision of their educational ministry.

Some small churches make this entire task the job of the Sunday school superintendent. That is both unfair and unfortunate. It is unfair because, even in the smallest church, the job is too much for one person to handle alone. It is unfair because it puts an individual on the spot by forcing him or her to make decisions alone that should reflect the best thoughts and ideas of the whole church. It is unfortunate because one person, no matter who that person is, cannot produce what several working together can, and consequently the church ends up with a poorer education ministry. It is also unfortunate for all the people who are never part of creating and carrying out that ministry. They miss the opportunity for the growth that occurs when you do this work, and the church is poorer for the lack of members who have done this growing. Therefore, it is important that a group, rather than an individual, have overall responsibility for educational ministry.

In summary, the important thing is, not which group does the job, but that some group knows it is responsible for the educational ministry of each church. That group needs to meet regularly enough to guarantee that it has time to give thoughtful supervision to the educational ministry of that church.

WARNING: Many churches have a ruling board that is officially charged with overseeing the spiritual growth of the congregation. In the Presbyterian Church it is the Session. In The United Methodist Church it is the Administrative Board. In the United Church of Christ it is the Board of Deacons. This board, whatever its name, is usually the highest official body in the local congregation, and therefore has a vast variety of responsibilities. Though it is officially charged with the job of spiritual growth, only in a rare case should that board be the responsible group described in this chapter. For one thing, these boards are too busy overseeing a variety of ministries to give in-depth work to any one of them. Furthermore, people elected to such boards are not chosen for their involvement in, or capability for, education work. Often these people must be educated about the value of various programs by those who are directly involved in them and leading them. Therefore, it is important that there be another "responsible group" to do the detailed work and in-depth explorations of education possibilities. It is also important that the responsible group understand its relationship to the ruling board. They must report decisions and clear plans as required by church law.

Assignments

(1) Read whatever document in your church describes how it shall be governed, in order to find out who is officially responsible for educational ministry in your church. Make a list of their specific duties to the educational ministry of the church.

(2) Find out who is "the responsible group" in your church. Who are the members of that group? How did they come to serve on it? How does it carry out its responsibilities?

(3) If there is no "responsible group" in your church, talk to your minister and ruling board about starting one. Then, initiate any action needed to get one organized and functioning.

Part Two:
The Church School

Education or spiritual growth is not limited to the church school. It is woven into every part of the church's life. Worship, mission, and fellowship all educate. There are many exciting new opportunities for spiritual growth being offered in churches today. Sunday school is being replaced by week-night classes. Families, instead of being divided into age group classes, are studying and worshiping together on family life retreats. Youth clubs are reaching more children in some communities than church school. Youth ministry is going on at church-sponsored teen discos.

But, especially in smaller churches, most serious opportunities for Christian growth are going to be directly tied to a Sunday morning church school. That time has traditionally been set apart by the church for such opportunities. A significant number of people still expect to be involved at the church in education at that hour. So for most small churches, providing a good education ministry begins with building a strong church school. For many of these churches, a strong church school can provide nearly all the opportunities needed.

Because of this, the majority of this book focuses on the church school. The twelve chapters of this part deal with specific tasks involved in setting up and maintaining the church school. Part 3 will offer some educational possibilities beyond church school.

One:

Why Do People Come to Church School at All?

People do not have to attend church school. That is obvious, because many do not. But many people do attend, some more regularly than others. They come because they choose to (unless their parents or a spouse is forcing them to come). Most come for very specific reasons. They come looking for or expecting something that may be very important to them. If you ask them why they come, they may tell you the real reason, or they may not. In either case, it is essential for the group responsible for education in their church to be aware of the reasons why people in that particular congregation come to church school, and what those people expect to find there.

You may agree or disagree with their motivations and expections, but the education ministry you offer must, in some way, respond to them. You may ignore their wishes to offer what you think they need. You may offer them exactly what they want, ignoring your own ideas. Or, you may plan to meet their desires in a way that goes beyond what they want or expect. But, because whatever you do will be a response to these reasons and expectations, it is important that you be conscious of the reasons that are motivating the people of your church.

Step One: Why Do You Come to Church School?

The pages at the end of this chapter contain descriptions of seven different reasons why people attend church school. Cut these pages out of the book, and cut each page in half along the dotted lines. You now have a collection of cards. Spread them on the table with the title side up (the side labeled "RESPONSE" will face down). Read through each description, and select the one or two that best describe your reasons for attending church school. If you are working with a group, take time to share your self-evaluations with each other.

SAMPLE: I, Carolyn Brown, am a blend of 50 percent scholar and 50 percent Christian Lifer. I'd have a hard time choosing between a class that was "really going to dig in" to some part of the Bible, and one that was going to explore some current issue I am concerned about from a Christian perspective. If I couldn't find a class that offered a good bit of at least one of these, I'd probably go looking for it somewhere else.

What do *you* look for in church school?

Step Two: What Motivates People at Your Church to Come to Church School?

Now think about the people in your church. What motivates them to come to church school? Obviously, no church will be made up of people who share identical motivations. In some churches, the majority may fall into two or three categories. But most churches will have representatives of every opinion listed. Your job is to identify who shares which opinions. To do that, spread the cards out. Note on each card the people or groups who come for that reason. For example, there may be a class of inspiration seekers meeting regularly. Write its name or some identification of it in the margin of the "INSPIRATION SEEKERS" card. Or you may know an individual who is a classic example of the ritualist. Write his or her name on that card. Don't forget the children and youth! You may recognize some reasons for coming to church school that are not included on the cards. Describe them on the extra card provided, and identify the people and groups who hold them.

DO NOT GET BOGGED DOWN! This step should take no more than ten minutes. You want an overall picture that is accurate, but not too detailed.

Finally, circle the name of every individual or group you think is getting what it wants.

Step Three: What Does Your Denomination Say About Motivation?

Many denominations or local churches have official stands on some of these reasons for attending church school. Presbyterian churches, for example, have a long history of emphasis on studying. A rallying cry of several years ago was, "Let the church school be the *school* of the church!" On the local level, some churches or church education committees of many denominations have decreed that youth will focus on Christian life concerns during church school. Youthful desires for fellowship are officially to be met elsewhere.

What are the official stands or preferences of your church and denomination? If necessary, ask your minister or some knowledgeable church leader for help on this. Note these stands on the appropriate card(s).

Step Four: How Do You Respond to All These Motivations?

Sometimes what people want and what people need are not the same. By now, you have probably identified at least one group that wants something that you, who have responsibility for education ministry, feel the church cannot or should not provide. What can you do?

(1) You can plan to provide what they want anyway. You can refuse to sit in judgment on the desires of others, especially if they are adults. You may realize that not meeting their needs will produce trouble and probably not lead these people to change, and therefore, for the sake of peace, you can give them what they want.

There are times at which this is the loving response. For example, a small class of elderly women who prize fellowship and inspiration can be provided a comfortable room and the necessary teacher, as a ministry of love. On the other hand, there are times when to give people what they want is not fulfilling your responsibility. The young adult class that enjoys just "shooting the bull" needs a firm challenge to get on to the business of growing in their faith.

(2) You can give them what *you* want in spite of what *they* want. This is almost guaranteed to produce trouble, even with young children. It is not advisable unless absolutely necessary. When it is necessary, it is best to be open and honest about what you are doing. For instance, announce that the ruling board has decided to discontinue opening assembly in order that individual classes can have more time for lessons, and then be ready to accept the anger of the ritualists. It will come. But at least they will know who made the decision and why. The anger can be focused on the proper issues and people.

(3) You can give them what they want in order to get them to accept what you believe they need. For example, the youth who have a high desire for fellowship can be offered a recreation and fellowship program Sunday evening, and encouraged to come to a study class with fellowship fringe benefits on Sunday morning.

(4) You can offer people more than they want by developing what they want to its fullest potential. This approach works very well in the church-school situation, because none of the reasons for attendance listed is totally and completely unacceptable. Each one has some shortsightedness, to be sure, but each also has some merit. If you can develop the part of the motivation that has merit, often the people will follow you to grow through it to deeper understanding and new motivation.

In each situation, you must decide which of these four approaches, or which combination of approaches, is the best response.

On the back of each card is a paragraph or two describing some possible response to people attending church school on the basis of that particular motivation. Read these responses and then refer to your notes on the front of the card to answer the following questions:

(1) How has our church responded to these people? Have our responses been appropriate?

(2) Particularly if many of the groups or individuals identified seem unsatisfied, what responses could we make to better encourage their growth?

Crucial Last Step

If this discussion has generated ideas about ways your church could respond more effectively to its members, make the plans to implement your ideas. Assign tasks and set a date to report on work done. Follow through. All your thought and discussion here will be worth little, unless you translate them into action in your church's education ministry.

THE SCHOLARS

These people believe that the job of the church school is to offer members of all ages opportunities to add to their understanding of the Bible, the creeds, and the theology of our faith. According to them, it is this understanding on which Christians base their individual and church lives. Therefore, it is essential for a church to set aside time specifically for increasing and deepening the understanding of the faith. These people come to church school to study.

PEOPLE WHO NEED PEOPLE

There are many people who come to church school simply to be with the people there. These include the junior high students who come because they prefer being with other junior high students to the boredom of Sunday morning at home, the rural young adults for whom this is one of the few chances to keep up with friends they have grown up with, and that group of men (or women) who would simply rather chew the fat than go to a class. For these people, being part of the Christian community is more valuable than the content of any lesson. It is this community that teaches and cares for the individual. And it is this community that gives meaning to life.

THE RITUALISTS

These people can be among the most regular attenders. They may never say a word, but you can count on their being there. Many of these people regard church school as a part of a total Sunday morning pattern that includes the worship service. It is the pattern or ritual that is important to them, rather than the content. The weekly repetition of hymns, lessons, and prayers may give their life a sense of order and security they treasure. Or they may go through the pattern to pay their dues or to make brownie points with God. Or they may just come out of habit. Whatever the underlying motive, the ritualists come to repeat the pattern.

RESPONSE

These people are scholars. Provide them with scholars' tools. Buy individual students' books. They will probably use them, keep them, and build a home Christian library they will treasure. Be sure dictionaries, commentaries, concordances, and other study tools, written on their level (scholars come in all ages), are available and used in their classes.

Some scholars enjoy classes in which everyone participates in research and discussion during class. Such students can take turns assuming the teaching role in an adult class, because they view the teacher more as an organizer of the day's work than as the expert. Other scholars however, want a TEACHER. If there is no excellent lay teacher in a church of many such students, it may be worth paying a seminary student or local professor to teach. Even a small church group of scholars can find the money to pay to get this teacher if it is really important.

Finally, scholars are usually interested in the basics, so the starting point of most classes should be scripture or some central church document. This may lead to discussion of current issues that are related, but the focus and starting point should not be the issues.

RESPONSE

Some groups of people have higher needs for fellowship than others. Churches need to identify those groups and provide opportunities beyond church school. Junior high students may need weekly fellowship groups. Young adults may need a couples' club. Single people may need a singles' group. Meeting these needs elsewhere can open the church school hour for other pursuits.

Church schools whose members are fellowship-oriented need coffee as well as curriculum. Add a fellowship time before church school. Offer coffee or whatever and a chance to visit. If necessary, put a pot in every adult class.

Provide a teacher who is loved by the particular students and knows the community well. Because of his or her position in and knowledge of the community, such a teacher can lead a class beyond fellowship to growing in understanding and living the faith. Often the best way to do this is to begin with personal life issues or community problems.

Generally, you do not need to provide pupils' books for such classes because they will not get used. Instead the teacher needs a leaders' guide and one copy of the pupil book.

There is a sub-group of the "people who need people" who are not going to be persuaded by any means to be part of any class. Somehow they are stuck at the church at church school time and will visit with others who share this situation. Provide this group a place to gather that does not distract the classes.

RESPONSE

Ritualists get what they want *in the established pattern*. They are likely to go along with a variety in content, so long as *the pattern* is not affected. If you are going to minister to these people, you need to begin by ministering within their established patterns.

There are two basic ways of adding new life and depth to church schools or classes of ritualists. (1) Go through the less productive parts of the pattern as efficiently as possible in order to open the largest possible time for teaching in freer ways. For example, if class *must* begin with a hymn and a devotional, limit this opening to five minutes. Encourage beginning promptly, and keep everything brief. Discourage singing all six verses of a hymn. This will give maximum teaching time while protecting the ritualists' commitment to the pattern. (2) Develop the ritual to its fullest potential. Make sure every part of it offers an opportunity for learning. For example, instead of limiting the opening worship as described above, develop it. Work hard to bring it to life. Experiment with a variety of kinds of devotionals. Try relating the devotion to the topic of the day's lesson, or use the devotion to dig deeper into the meaning of the hymn. Most patterns have the potential to have meaningful content. With some work, the pattern that satisfies the ritualist can become interesting to others too. It is also possible to catch the attention of the ritualists and call them to growing beyond appreciation of the ritual.

One last thing about confirmed ritualists. Do not ask them to be part of planning or giving direction to a new education ministry. They do not have new ideas. Rather, ask them to take some part within the pattern that sustains them.

CHRISTIAN LIFERS

Many people are hungry for an opportunity to explore how the Christian faith relates to their everyday life and the issues of today's world. Adults are forced into ethical dilemmas in their businesses and are perplexed by the maze of local, national, and international issues that demand their response. Teenagers are dealing with peer pressure, decisions about their futures, and the same "BIG" issues that perplex adults. Children want help relating to people and understanding the world. These people insist that church school studies must be *relevant* to these everyday problems. A class that does not have something to say about these pressing problems is meaningless, according to these people.

CLASS MEMBERS

Some people expect their church school class to be a miniature of the church. They expect to worship, be involved in outreach projects, take care of each other, and study together in their class. They expect birthday cards from the class and visits from classmates when they are ill. They may spend most of a class session planning a class social or arranging to take fruit baskets to the church's shut-ins. Membership in their particular class may be as important to them as their membership in the church. (Again, these people are found in every age group.)

THE GRADUATES

These people believe the church school is primarily for children. Its task is to teach children the basics of the faith, so that they will graduate to be Christians and good church members. It is their opinion that preaching replaces church school for graduated adults. They get all the input they want from the sermon. If other adults are interested in further study, that is fine. However, most graduates are not and do not appreciate being pressured to join a class.

RESPONSE

These people are generally anxious to participate in planning their own classes. A class of Christian lifers can be counted on to select their own study topics. Often they will be willing to rotate teaching responsibilities. Because there is no one curriculum that satisfies Christian lifers, a class of them will go through an enormous amount of resources. However, these will more often be kits, pamphlets, filmstrips, and speakers, than pupil books. If someone does some homework, many of these resources for group use can be obtained or borrowed free from community libraries and interest groups. So, instead of buying a set of teachers' and students' quarterlies, you may want to buy a kit, rent a movie to go with free literature, and provide funds for speakers. Your cost for the quarter should come out nearly even or cheaper in the end.

RESPONSE

The response to these people depends on the church. In some very small churches, the church school does, and indeed must, carry on many of the functions listed. It is the only organized group available to respond to personal needs within the congregation and initiate outreach efforts. In these churches, classes need to recognize their many functions and organize to carry them out as efficiently as possible.

In other churches, a class trying to be a mini-church is duplicating and occasionally in conflict with other groups to which tasks are assigned. In such situations, a teacher who is a strong leader, and who understands the situation, is most helpful. Such a leader can direct the activities of class members. Part of this direction can include streamlining activities, such as sending cards so that they take minimum class time, and expanding other activities so that they become more meaningful. For example, instead of simply planning to visit a nursing home one Sunday afternoon, the teacher could lead the class into a unit of study on the needs of the aging and ways the church has ministered and can minister to the elderly. Such a study might lead to other class projects that involve deeper commitment and understanding. In that way, a class project becomes a learning/growing experience. In undertaking such projects, the teacher needs to be in communication with other groups within the church to avoid duplication or conflict.

RESPONSE

An influential minister or church leader can sometimes point out the need for adults to continue learning about, and growing in, their faith. He or she might thus convince graduates that they are missing something. So ask your minister to preach on this subject and to personally challenge the graduates in your congregation.

If efforts to educate graduates into continued learning fail, the only way to get them involved in church school is to involve them in providing for the children. Concentrate on building an excellent children's class with their help. Ask them to help buy or build equipment and set up the children's class. Enlist them as teachers. Make sure they get some good training for the job. They will grow in their understanding of our faith as they teach. (Remember the old adage about the teacher learning more than the students.)

INSPIRATION SEEKERS

These people want church school to be an inspirational hour. They look forward to a time when someone else takes responsibility for feeding them insights and ideas that "lift them up" and enable them to find some sense and beauty in their world. For them, church school is an extension of the worship hour. It is a haven from the difficulties of daily life. It is a time to be reassured that God is still in control and that the old definitions of right and wrong still stand. Some inspiration seekers are people who are fighting losing battles daily. They come looking for renewed vision to give them the strength to carry on.

OTHERS YOU RECOGNIZE IN YOUR CHURCH

RESPONSE

Because inspiration seekers are waiting "to be fed," they often insist on passive roles in church school. A class full of them almost requires a teacher who will give an inspirational lecture/lesson followed by time for limited discussion each week. This becomes nearly a ritual pattern for them.

Because many small churches have enough of these adults to make it possible to have a class especially for them, this is often the easiest and best approach. All that is necessary for such a class is a willing lecturer of similar persuasion. Pupils' books may not even be necessary, unless "reading the lesson" is part of the ritual.

There is, however, need for some loving discernment here. Some inspiration seekers do need simple support. Others need a challenge. They have selected one usually narrow point of view and are defending it vehemently. They come to hear that point of view supported and to be inspired in their valiant fight. These latter inspiration seekers may benefit more from participating in the give-and-take of heated discussions between loving Christians of different persuasions. The best response may be to offer these people mostly such opportunities in church school, IF you can assure that there will be lots of love and support given with the challenge.

RESPONSE

Two:

Who Does What?

In even the smallest church, good Christian education does not just happen. Plans for programs and curricula must be thoughtfully prepared. Leaders must be enlisted. The heat must be turned on or the windows opened. People must be notified of times and places and be encouraged to attend. The list goes on to include a grand variety of major jobs and mechanical tasks, each of which is important to the success of the ministry. Someone or some group must have clear responsibility for each item on the list.

If clear responsibility is not assigned, either the job goes undone, or some faithful workhorse sees the need and steps in. Neither of these alternatives is productive. If the job is not done, obviously a less-than-desired ministry results. If a workhorse steps in, someone has been abused. Eventually workhorses grow tired of accepting all the unsolicited tasks, or they accept so many that their load becomes a burden. In either case, they retire leaving jobs no one will attempt to fill because they are so huge and ill-defined.

All that is needed to avoid these pitfalls is a clear, public definition of who does what in your church's education ministry. Again, there is no one right way to assign these tasks, only the way that works in your church. The organization suggested by your denomination may be helpful, but it need not put restrictions on you. For example, if there is someone with training and interest in maintaining all the audio-visual equipment, assign him or her that job instead of assigning it to a particular officer, who may or may not have the necessary interest and talent.

What is important is not that "the proper person" do each job but that each job be clearly assigned to someone. The remainder of this chapter describes a process that enables "the responsible group" to identify every task and the person or group responsible for carrying out that task.

Step One: Identifying the Jobs to Be Done

The following pages are divided into six cards each. Cut the pages out of the book and cut each page along the dotted lines. You now have thirty cards. Each card describes one job necessary to the smoothly operating education ministry.

The last page of this chapter is also to be cut into sections along the dotted lines. Each of these cards names one person or group that may be responsible for part of the church's education work. If some of these do not exist in your church, discard the appropriate card(s). One blank card is included for you to fill in the names of other individuals or groups that are at work in your church. Make other cards if you need them.

Step Two: Matching People and Jobs

Spread all the cards out on a table. Working together, match each job with the person or group responsible. If you find jobs that do not apply to your situation, discard them. For example, if you do not have an opening assembly, you will not need to assign someone to prepare and lead them. But be careful about discarding jobs. Be sure you are not avoiding or overlooking some ministry that should be done. You may also be aware of some task that is not included on these cards. If so, write it on another piece of paper and add it. It is important that every job be included.

Step Three: Evaluating Job Assignments

Once you have matched each job with a person or group, look at the arrangement.

- Is any person or group overloaded?
- Is any office or group unnecessary?
- Are individuals and groups doing tasks appropriate to them?

As you identify problems, begin reshuffling tasks as necessary. You may want to create a new office or assign two people to fill one office. For example, if the superintendent's list is too long for one person, consider appointing an assistant superintendent or two co-superintendents. You could assign each person specific jobs, or simply let them divide the work as they wish.

You may want to eliminate an office for which there is no real purpose.

Step Four: Preserving Job Assignments

When you are satisfied with the way you have assigned the necessary jobs, preserve your work. List on paper the job(s) assigned to each person or group.

<u>EXAMPLE</u>

The superintendent shall:
1. keep attendance records
2. order curriculum for all classes
3. hear teachers' joys, problems, and sorrows
4. plan and lead opening assembly.

The teachers will:
1. plan lessons
2. attend workshops

etc.

You now have a job description for everyone involved in your education ministry. Make plans to (1) preserve them, and (2) make them public knowledge.

(1) Do whatever is necessary to preserve your work. Put the job descriptions in the education file. Post them on the wall in some appropriate place. Record them in your minutes. Each church has its own way of keeping up with such things. What is important is that these lists of responsibilities be readily available. They can be used in enlisting teachers and officers. In chapter 6 you will use these lists to create covenants for teachers. The lists become a checklist for an efficient program. They can determine to whom new tasks are assigned. So do not lose them.

(2) Make the lists public. Tasks are often left undone because no one is sure to whom the job belongs. Rather than risk "taking over" and possibly hurting someone's feelings, people let jobs go. Or, out of fear that doing it once will saddle them with it for a lifetime, people leave needed work undone. These and similar problems are avoided if "who does what" is public knowledge. If you have an annual directory, print job descriptions there. Print them in your newsletter. Call a meeting of all involved to review the lists and accept them. Post them in some appropriate place. Do whatever is necessary to make sure all people doing education work and the people in the congregation know to whom different tasks are assigned.

Provide substitutes

Prepare and lead opening assembly

Plan lessons

Plan annual events like Rally Day, Christmas Program, etc. List below any events to be planned for your church.

Hear the teachers'
—needs
—problems
—joys
—sorrows

Plan and provide publicity for the education ministry.

Select and evaluate curriculum used in all classes

Keep attendance records

Count and deposit the offering

Oversee youth fellowship(s)

Recruit teachers/leaders for education ministry

Plan for Communicants' Classes as necessary

Create a learning atmosphere with posters, banners, bulletin boards, furniture arrangement, etc.

Plan and oversee the budget for the church's education ministry.

Enroll new students

Be sure that each group or class has a CLEAN, WARM place to meet.

Compile class rolls. Figure out who should be included in each class or group. (Each roll should include names, addresses, and phone numbers.)

Search out missing students. Encourage them (in appropriate ways) to attend.

Be sure that all necessary
record players
tape recorders
filmstrip projectors
movie projectors
are available and working

Buy and keep on hand basic supplies:
- pencils
- crayons
- paper
- scissors
- glue
- etc.

Be able to operate all audio-visual equipment at the church

Buy unusual supplies for special projects

EXAMPLE: colored cellophane for making stained glass windows in the children's class.

Select and buy class resources such as Bible dictionaries, classroom Bibles, maps, etc.

Order curriculum so that each class has the right number of the right books at the right time.

Take advantage of leader-training programs in your own church and in your area.

Buy subscriptions to magazines for teachers.

Be sure that leaders and teachers have enough training to do their jobs well.

Decide which books are added to the church library and oversee its operation.

Pay for and/or
provide transportation
Provide child care

to enable teachers and leaders to attend workshops.

Be sure that every class has a teacher every Sunday.

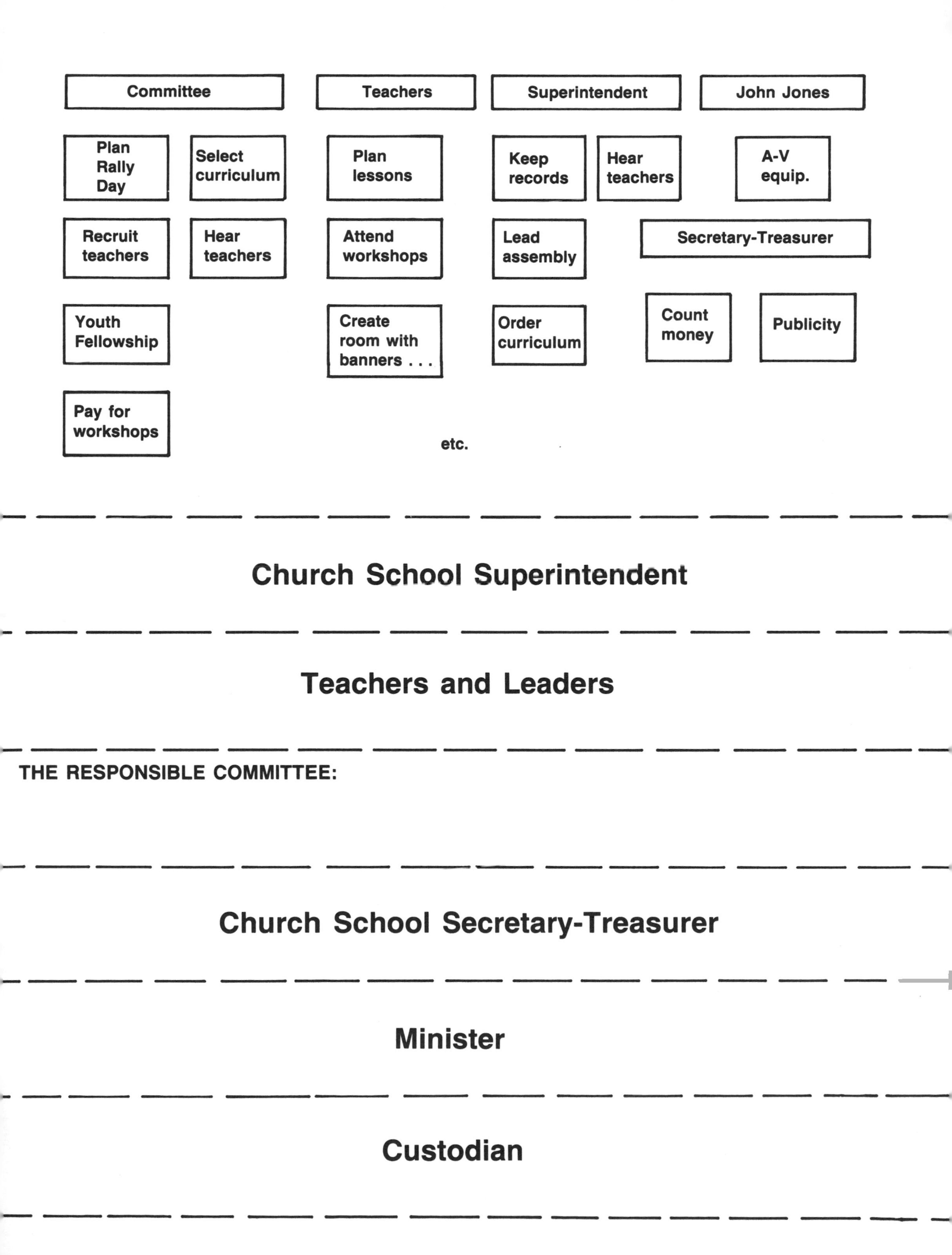
Committee
Teachers
Superintendent
John Jones
Plan Rally Day
Select curriculum
Plan lessons
Keep records
Hear teachers
A-V equip.
Recruit teachers
Hear teachers
Attend workshops
Lead assembly
Secretary-Treasurer
Youth Fellowship
Create room with banners . . .
Order curriculum
Count money
Publicity
Pay for workshops
etc.
Church School Superintendent
Teachers and Leaders
THE RESPONSIBLE COMMITTEE:
Church School Secretary-Treasurer
Minister
Custodian

Three:

Dividing for Classes

Public schools group children in classes pretty much according to age. Most church school curricula are packaged for classes of ten to fifteen students of approximately the same age. Therefore, we often assume that the "best" church-school classes include ten to fifteen students of approximately the same age. When the students are children, this means no more than two or three years' difference in ages. The youth class may include a three- to four-year age span. But even the adults can be subdivided into younger adults and older adults. The assumption is that people learn best with others of the same age. Accepting this assumption, we in small churches often hopelessly dream of the day when our church will grow large enough to provide really good education—or we give up on doing any real quality education at all because "we are so very small."

False Assumption #1: People Learn Best with Others of the Same Age

This may be true in our public schools, because they are trying to teach very specific skills and pass on certain sets of facts. But we in our churches are less interested in preparing students to pass standardized tests on the facts about Christianity, than we are in leading students ever deeper into the Christian life. Therefore, an eleventh grader sharing her response to cheating with a seventh grader, or a sixth grader discussing the problems between Jacob and Esau, in a class that includes his second-grade brother, may be far more productive than anything done in closely graded classes. In short, good Christian education is not limited to classes of the same age. Good Christian education happens whenever people are challenged to explore some part of their faith.

False Assumption #2: It Takes Ten Students to Form a Good Class

Good Christian education does not even require classes of ten students each. Unfortunately, many people have the idea that smaller classes are less interesting and not worth the effort. It is true that a class of three or four will be less likely to have outside speakers, spend $25 to rent a movie, or include as wide a variety of opinions on a subject that a class of fifteen would. But it is also true that each of the three or four students will participate more fully and be able to more completely explore their own particular questions than would the students in the class of fifteen. In one small church, there is a class of "Christian lifers" whose average attendance is five. The other adult class of twelve "ritualists" and "scholars" does not understand why the five do not give up and join them. But the students in the little class are growing together in a way they could not grow in the larger class. They are in the best possible class for them.

The question of whether a class of less than ten is really worth it is a product of our big-numbers-oriented world. We are pushed to be "the biggest" and reach "the most." In the face of this pressure, we must constantly remind ourselves that we serve a Lord who places high value on the individual. Jesus told parables about a shepherd who left the ninety-nine to find a single sheep, a woman searching for one coin, and a father waiting for one lost son. He promised his presence wherever two or three—not ten to fifteen—are gathered in his name. We have biblical insistence that teaching two or three is just as important as teaching fifteen. Therefore, we must do whatever is necessary to remind ourselves and others of that.

In summary, we must set aside these assumptions about the size of classes and the way to group people for education. We must free ourselves to create education groups that are appropriate to the people in our churches.

Small churches are especially able to do this, because in small churches every student is known as a person. So, instead of facing twenty first graders, sixteen second graders, eleven third graders, and so forth; we plan for shy Tommy in the first grade, Jennifer and Sandy who are best buddies in the third grade, and John Allen who, at four years old, is as active as he is brilliant. Because we know our students personally, we can plan for classes that respond to the special needs and interests of each one.

Because we are small, we can be more flexible in the ways we respond to them. For example, one year a mature sixth grader may be included in the youth class. Another sixth grader in another year may belong in the children's class. Yet another child may happily start her sixth-grade year in the children's class. By March, having grown two inches, gotten a sleek new haircut, and now dreaming of being a cheerleader, she may need to move into the youth class. If fifth-grade Lisa and seventh-grade Jo Ann are inseparable friends, we can plan for them to be included in the same classes. Larger churches have to set standard patterns because so many people are involved. Smaller churches are free to respond to the individual.

Some Ways to Divide Classes

There are many ways of grouping people for classes.

(1) *By age:* Though closely graded classes are not necessary, groups of approximately the same age often benefit from learning together. In many small churches this may indicate the need for three classes: a children's class, a youth class, and an adult class. The boundaries between the classes can be vaguely defined to allow individuals to move from one to another when they are ready.

Inevitably, however, there will be one or two individuals who are isolated by their age. The children's class, for example, may include a cluster of kindergarten through second-grade children and one fifth grader. When this fifth grader is twelve, the next older person is fifteen. The next younger person is eight. Again, the individual's needs and interests determine how he is placed. Often it is possible to group him with the younger children as a teacher's helper. The teacher can offer him chances to learn by leading. It is especially educational if the teacher includes the young helper in planning his leadership role in a few special projects.

Another approach to the lone student is to provide single-person learning projects. In one small church, a bright twelve-year-old was provided with her very own desk and a self-instruction workbook (there are several such workbooks available through most church-school supply companies). For several months she was delighted to work her way through a very thorough survey of the Bible. The teacher of the younger children checked in with her at the end of each session and helped out when necessary. Such an arrangement would not be satisfactory on a long-term basis, but it is a good short-term option.

Finally, it is at times necessary to simply decide whether this particular person will be better off as a student in the younger or in the older group. If there is no clear choice, it may be better to move him into the older group because many children, who would stop coming if put with "the babies," will rise to unexpected heights in order to make it in the older class.

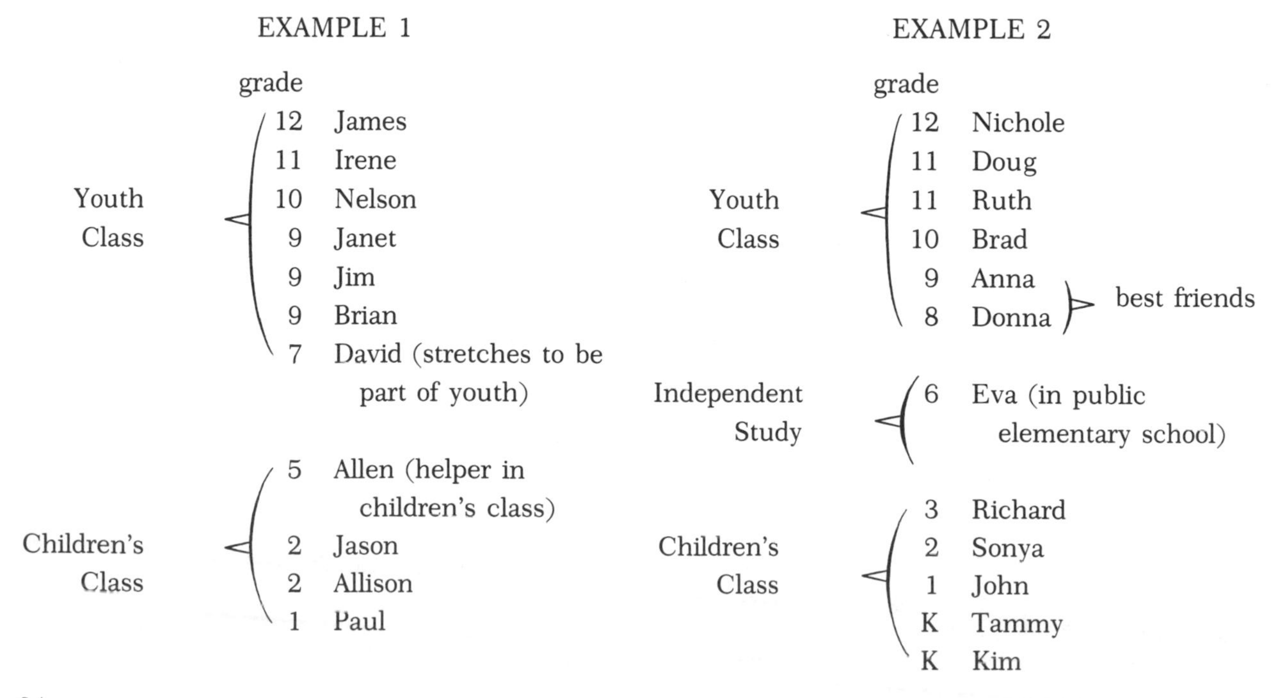

(2) *By friendship groups:* Some classes are already formed. They simply need to be recognized. For example, a group of children who live near each other and attend school together may be so strongly tied to each other that they may need to move through church school as a group. It will not matter whether they are labeled children or youth, as long as they are together. There are similar groups among adults.

(3) *By sex:* Years ago, all church-school classes were divided along sex lines. Most churches abandoned them in order to provide interaction and discussion between the sexes. Few of us would want a permanent return to divided classes. But occasionally groups of males or females can learn together and share in unique ways.

One year a church divided the children's class into a girl's class and a boy's class. Women taught the girls, and men taught the boys. The girls, all music-lovers, concentrated on studying hymns and learning new Christian songs. They sang at a nursing home and during the church's worship service on several occasions. The boys, meanwhile, were studying the heroes of the Bible, raking the yards of some shut-in members of the church, and taking in a pro-ball game. Granted, this sounds like sexism, but for one year it was a very special way to group people to learn together.

(4) *By motivation:* Chapter 1 described in detail several reasons why people attend church school and the ways those reasons can affect classes. It is often possible to group people into classes according to their motivation.

(5) *Intergenerational groups:* Very few groups would choose to learn in intergenerational groups on a regular, long-term basis. But many groups enjoy learning this way occasionally. Seasonal events are especially suited for this. For example, during low attendance in the summer, many churches replace regular classes with a series of classes designed to include people of all ages. One church asked a different family to take responsibility for planning and leading each session of the summer months. A box full of appropriate resources was provided for their use. The Advent-Christmas season is another appropriate time for intergenerational events. Church-wide projects, such as decorating Jesse trees or Christmas trees, can keep students of all ages working and learning together during the month of December.

By now, you may be recognizing other ways of dividing people into classes in your church. That's great! Once again, there is no right or wrong way, but only the ways that work, or do not work, for you.

Dividing Your Students for Classes

Step One: List your students

Make a list of all the students (children and adults) who are in any way involved in the church school. Beside each of the children's names, write their grade in school or their age (if they are preschoolers). If possible, arrange the children's names in chronological order. Star (★) the names of people who attend regularly.

Step Two: Brainstorm possible classes

Study your list to answer the following questions:

—What natural groups among the students suggest possible class divisions?

—How could you divide . . . by age?
. . . by friendship pattern?
. . . by sex?
. . . by motivation?
. . . others?

—In what situations would intergenerational learning be appropriate?

Step Three: Choose the best one(s)

Select the division of classes that seems most appropriate for your church at this time. Identify seasons or special events for which you might try different groups.

Step Four: Preserve your list

Save your list of students and classes, but do not carve them into stone. What looks like the perfect class arrangement now, may be most inappropriate in a year or even less. Your openness and flexibility were the key to planning these classes. They will be the key to keeping classes appropriate. So save the list as a starting point for your next reorganization. But stay open-minded, because everything changes.

For example, in September a bright five-year-old was the youngest in a children's class that included all children through sixth grade. The class was moving along fairly smoothly, until a three-year-old joined in November. That made the class unmanageable. The five-year-old, the three-year-old, and a shy second grader (all regular attenders) were given a teacher and their own class. The new class made both classes manageable and gave the second grader a chance to shine as a leader in the younger group. This happy rearrangement was possible because some responsible people were keeping up with the class and were ready to rearrange their plans to respond to the changing situation.

Four:

Broadly Graded Classes for Small-Church Children

I have already spoken against the assumption that the best Christian education is done in closely graded classes. But the fact is that most small churches are forced into broadly graded classes. If there are only ten children between the ages of four and twelve, one children's class may be the only option. When I speak of broadly graded classes, I am referring to classes that may include children in grades 1–6 and even a preschool child or two, or classes that include youth in grades 6–12. Far from being an unfortunate last resort, these classes offer a number of advantages, if a few key guidelines are followed.

Advantages in Broadly Graded Classes

First of all, the church is a community, or family. Children are becoming part of the family by sharing in its work, worship, and fun, and by learning its story and values. Therefore, the best "education" will take place in family-like settings. Broadly graded classes provide this. Younger children "learn the ropes" from the older ones. For example, a fifth grader quickly taught a third-grade teammate how to use the table of contents in the Bible in order to speed up their work on a class game. That third grader would have learned the skill less eagerly from an adult teacher.

The "family setting" of broadly graded classes allows for some close-to-home heroes. The younger children have a chance to get to know "the big kids," to admire their skills and appreciate their attention. They get some Christian kids to look up to and imitate. The "big kids" get the joy of being heroes and a chance to fill their hero-shoes responsibly. They have more opportunities to learn to be leaders than they would with a group their own age. Relationships built here carry over to other places. For example, when fearful five-year-old Brian got on the school bus, he was greeted by fifth-grade Tony from his church-school class. Tony had promised to keep an eye on Brian as he learned the ways of school buses.

A final advantage is that broadly graded classes force us to share our faith in less academic ways. Because our students have greatly varying reading and writing skills, we are challenged to find ways to avoid using those skills exclusively. Generally, that leads to more active, human learning, which is more in keeping with the Christian faith.

Keys to Success

Many people avoid broadly graded teaching because they associate it with unstructured classrooms, learning centers, and other "experimental" ideas. It can be, but does not have to be. Unless your children are involved in these kinds of learning situations in school, it is not advisable to try them in church school. But not using learning centers does not rule out the possibility of a successful broadly graded class. Remember, the one-room schoolhouse was a broadly graded class!

There are a few keys to success.

1 Plan a variety of activities. Most sessions need to include several different activities in order to keep the attention and interest of all the children. The attention span of young children can be very short. So teachers need to be ready with a series of related brief activities. One session might include hearing a story, acting it out in simple costumes, learning a related song, and composing a group prayer related to the theme of the story. Dramatic activities work particularly well in broadly graded classes, because each student can enter into them from her own level. Therefore, while every student in a class of fifth graders will want to be the star, a broadly graded class provides a supply of younger children willing to cherish smaller parts.

2 Work in a variety of groups. Many activities can be done by the whole group: singing, dramatics, viewing filmstrips, hearing stories, planning class projects, playing learning games. However, it is often necessary to divide the class. Students may be paired up, with an older child and younger child working as partners. For example, they may be assigned to read a given verse of scripture and make a collage about it. The older child would have to take the lead in the looking up and reading, but they could work as equals on the collage.

It is also possible to divide by age for some activities. In this way, older children can be challenged to use their more advanced skills. While older children read a story from the Bible and work a crosswood puzzle requiring the use of their Bibles, younger children might hear the story and draw pictures of some part of it for a box TV.

At times, the group may be divided according to interest. A child is then offered the choice of telling a given story by painting a mural, using puppets, or making a box TV show. Offering such choices gives children a chance to make their own decisions about how they will learn.

Occasionally, a teacher may plan to divide the class, assigning children to specific groups in order to insure effective groups. If, for instance, you plan a game at which older children will excel, you may pre-plan the teams so they will be as evenly matched as possible.

A session will sometimes be carried out entirely in one of the above groups. But most often, it will be important to combine several groupings. For example, the class may begin together by listening to a recorded Bible story. For ten minutes, students could work in age groups to explore the meaning of the story. The majority of the session might be spent in interest groups. They could turn the story into a play by (1) writing a script, (2) painting scenery, and (3) making some props. Finally, the group would rejoin to put on their play.

Even small, broadly graded groups require at least two teachers planning together and present in the classroom every Sunday. The need for variety in activities and grouping demands it. One teacher simply cannot help two groups do two different activities at the same time. At first, the need for two teachers may look like a drawback. However, if you divide the children into classes that can be taught by a single teacher, you will need at least two teachers anyway. Each of these teachers will work alone. If a broadly graded class is formed, the two teachers will plan and teach together. Sharing the work in this way is both more enjoyable and rewarding for most teachers and more effective for the students.

4 Think about each student, and know what you want each one to gain from being part of the class. Then try to give them that. There is a vast difference in what a sixth grader expects and needs from church school and what a four-year-old expects and needs. They can both be satisfied in the same class if their teacher is intentionally planning for each of them. A sixth grader can deal with where an event occurred, how it was possible, how people responded then, and what it means to us today. A four-year-old is concerned with its meaning today and interested in the event if it makes a good story. But, mainly, a four-year-old needs to experience the church as a loving, interesting, happy place to be. Therefore a sixth grader may plan the script for the walls of Jericho play, paint boxes like stones to build a proper wall, discuss a fitting battle cry for when the walls fall, and be a lead soldier, while the four-year-old hears the story, paints a little on a box-stone, wanders around watching other preparations, gets a costume, and is one of the Israelites marching and screaming with delight when the wall falls. Both go home happy and with their needs met. If the teacher realizes this, he or she need not worry that the four-year-old was not involved in learning situations appropriate to that age level during one hundred percent of the session.

Select the curriculum carefully. There are few ongoing curriculum resources designed for broadly graded children's classes. Instead, you must select a curriculum designed for a closely graded class that is most appropriate to your particular group. Choose a curriculum aimed at the majority of your students. For a class of mainly younger children, select a curriculum for grades 1–3, or something similar. If your students tend to be clustered around one grade, select materials for that grade. As a general rule, it is better to select curriculum that is a little too old rather than one that is too young, because it is easier to adapt teaching activities "down" than "up."

	EXAMPLE	
	5th	Jane
	3d	Elizabeth
Select "Primary" or "Grade 2"	3d	Eric
	2nd	Andrew
	1st	Annie
	1st	Nicky
	K	Sam

Select a curriculum aimed at central age of class.

	EXAMPLE	
	6th	Diane
	5th	George
	5th	Ginger
Select "Grade 4"	4th	Sandy
	4th	Chris
	4th	Lee
	4th	Denis
	3d	Joe
	3d	Janice
	2nd	Sonya

Choose a curriculum aimed at a cluster of children.

If possible, look at several different curricula. Choose one that is less academic. Books that suggest games, dramas, and artistic learning activities are more successful in broadly graded classes than those that require a lot of reading and writing.

When these five keys are used, many small churches find that broadly graded classes open the door to excellent opportunities for their children and youth to grow in their understanding of their faith.

Assignments

(1) Review your list of children and youth. How could they be grouped for broadly graded classes? What advantages over your present divisions would such a grouping offer?

(2) If such a class looks like a possibility for your church, plan an experiment. Set up the class for at least a three-month trial. Evaluate it as the class progresses.

Five:

Selecting a Curriculum

There was a time when selecting a curriculum was easy. A church simply ordered whatever the denomination offered or endorsed. But that day is past. Today, a variety of curricula is being produced by individual denominations, groups of denominations, independent publishers, and individual authors. Churches are using some of all of them. Baptists are using Methodist pieces. Methodists are selecting some Roman Catholic studies. Twelve Protestant denominations have joined forces to produce a curriculum that is really four curricula to be mixed-and-matched by local congregations. And all denominations are benefitting from the work of creative leaders in the area of Christian education.

The big problems in the face of this variety are (1) how to keep up with what is available, and (2) how to select materials that are appropriate for your particular situation. In the face of these problems, small churches, especially, may decide to pass. It may be easier to keep getting what you have been using and ignore all the others. In some cases, that is the only reasonable decision. If you find yourself in such a situation, skip this chapter. But if you do want to explore some of this feast of materials, prepare for some hard but interesting work.

Who Selects the Curriculum?

The practice in many small churches is to let anyone who is willing to teach select his or her own materials. The church may provide a basic study book, but will leave teachers free to add to it, or even substitute anything else they can find. Most churches, however, have constitutional requirements about who selects, or at least approves, all materials used in the church school. There are good reasons for this. For one thing, the church school is charged with helping people grow in their faith. The materials used will, to a large extent, determine the direction of that growth. That direction is far too precious to leave without careful supervision. Second, in directing that growth there is a need for a long-range plan, as well as for short-range plans. We need a long-range plan to insure that students are dealing with all parts of the faith. Unless there is a plan, we may discover that our teen-agers have studied a great deal about the New Testament, but know nothing about the Old. Or they may know their Bible, but have no idea of the story of the church or how the church operates. Unless there is a long-range plan, the adult class may stick to a few favorite topics and avoid struggling with difficult concerns.

Individual teachers, no matter how genuine their concern, cannot provide all that is needed in selecting a church school curriculum. There must be some group that evaluates all the curriculum to be sure it meets the standards of the church and fits into a long-range curriculum plan.

So, *STEP ONE is to find out who that group is*. Your minister should be able to help you. In all likelihood, it will be the same group as the "responsible group" described in Part 1. This group may want to include others in making curriculum decisions. For example, teachers who will be using the materials may appreciate having a voice in their selection. Parents of young students may also want to be included. Some youth and adult students might even be included. The responsible group can include as many of these as possible in the process, but it is the committee that must make final decisions and insist that the materials they have chosen be used.

Finding Out What Is Available

This may be one of the hardest parts of the process for small churches. But it is possible to find out what curriculum resources are available. Sources for this information include . . .

A Knowledgeable Person.

Most denominations and publishing houses send out free catalogs and lots of advertising. You may be able to locate some person who keeps up with what is available and can share this information with you. If your minister is particularly interested in education, he or she may already have a file of such information and may be familiar with some of the materials. If not, you will need to find someone who does. Your conference, association, presbytery, or district may have a person on its staff who would be available to show you available materials. A Christian educator serving a nearby church may be willing to show you materials he or she knows of.

Do not hesitate to ask these people for help. Simply tell them, as specifically as possible, what you are looking for. If you want materials for a youth class mainly of boys who hate academic classes, say so. If you are looking for one curriculum that is Bible-centered for the whole church to follow in each class, say so. In response to your request, a Christian educator can lend you samples of materials or catalogs of materials to look through. Some companies will send copies of their materials for a ten-day free preview on your request.

A Resource Center.

If you are especially fortunate, there may be a church resource center in your area. These centers are libraries of Christian education materials. Some loan their materials. Others require that you evaluate them at the center. In this latter case, it is often possible to make an appointment for your committee to look through what the center has to offer in a given area with the help of a center staffperson. Such centers are usually sponsored by a district, presbytery, association, denomination, or a church college or seminary. Ask someone on your area denominational staff if there are such centers in your area and how you can use them.

A Local Bookstore.

Another way of discovering what is available is to visit a religious bookstore. This, however, must be done with caution. Most religious bookstores are operated by Christians who are selling books that reflect their particular theological position. In the case of denominationally run bookstores, this position is no secret. No Roman Catholic is going to go to a Baptist Bible bookstore expecting to find useful (to them) study materials on the sacrament of baptism, any more than a Baptist would expect to find such materials in a Catholic bookstore.

It is not so obvious what the position of an independent bookstore is. However, it is usually easy to find out. Your minister may be able to tell you. If not, ask salespeople if the store is connected to any denomination. If the answer is no, ask what church the owner attends. This will give you a clue. If the general theology of that church is very different from your own, do not flee the store, but do evaluate very carefully any material that you consider using. You can find some very usable maps, flannelgraphs, pictures, etc. You may also find some games, study books, songbooks, etc. that look fine on the surface, but will be unacceptable when you get into the content. So select carefully.

Assignment

To find out how *you* can learn about church school materials, get answers to the following questions:

(1) Is there a person on your denomination's area staff who will help people in local churches select their curriculum? If so, who is this person? How do you get his or her services? (Ask your minister, or call your denomination's area office.)

(2) Is there a resource center in your area? If so, where is it, and how can it be used by your church? (Again, your minister or denominational office can probably help you.)

(3) What kinds of Christian bookstores are in your area? Which ones might be useful sources of church-school materials for your church? (Identify stores by using the Yellow Pages of local phone books. Send people out to investigate any that are unfamiliar. Your minister or a church educator may know of a particularly good store that is worth a trip to a nearby city.)

Picking and Choosing

Once you become aware of what is available, the problem is choosing the materials that are right for your particular congregation. This task requires more than just flipping through the materials, but less than reading the entire book(s) in detail. There are three things to be evaluated in each piece of curriculum.

TEST #1—THE MESSAGE: Every resource has a message about the Christian faith and life. It proclaims its message in written words, the pictures it uses, the examples offered in lessons and suggested teaching activities. To decide about using a resource, you must know what its message is.

If a resource is part of a total curriculum, a statement of that message may be available. These statements are generally printed on a cover page or in the introduction to any leaders' book. More detailed statements can often be ordered, but for most purposes, the paragraph in the introduction of the book or in a catalog may provide sufficient informaton. If such a statement is available, read it.

Next, look at the table of contents. Read the titles of each session. Ask yourself how well the lesson subjects seem to cover the topic of the whole course. If, for example, you are evaluating a course on witnessing for Jesus and find that all the sessions deal with talking about your faith, while none mentions witnessing by action, you have learned that one message of the course is that witnessing is verbal. If you disagree with this position, you should seriously question using this course. So, read the table of contents to learn the outline of the message of the course.

Finally, read one or two lessons. (I usually avoid the first and last lessons, but choose a lesson or two at random from the middle. If the title of any lesson worries me, I always choose it.) As you read, watch for specific messages and between-the-lines messages. If a lesson titled "The Church Is the People of God" includes pictures of only white people in pretty clothes, there is a powerful between-the-lines message. If the only suggested activity in an adult study on serving God by serving the community is to take fruit baskets to invalid church members, there is a between-the-lines message about how we serve God. So, read carefully all the materials related to one or two sessions to learn about their messages.

Reading introductory paragraphs, the table of contents, and one or two lessons can give you a clear idea of the message of a church school resource. If you are evaluating books published by your own denomination, you may not need to be too cautious in this. But if you are evaluating the products of another denomination or of an independent publisher, it is important to be thorough. Be especially careful when evaluating the work of independent publishers, because they are not bound by the standards of any church body. It is especially important to identify their messages about salvation and the Christian life. What do they say is "saving" about Jesus Christ? And what do they say is distinctive about the Christian life? Christians look like any other nice, respectable, good citizens, in some curricula. Few churches would consciously teach this. Evaluate carefully.

TEST #2—TEACHING SUGGESTIONS: There are many ways of teaching and learning in church school. Some students sit in rows to listen to a teacher lecture. Some sit in circles to read and discuss together. Some move all around their rooms, working puzzles, producing plays, researching biblical ideas, planning class projects, creating banners, and so forth. Curriculum materials are designed with a particular one of these styles in mind. You need to identify that style and evaluate its appropriateness for your situation.

To do this, look again at the one or two lessons you have read. Picture in your mind a class doing this lesson at your church. Could it be done in your space, with your equipment, within your time, with your number of particular students and teachers? This does not mean you should ignore any curriculum that will require some changes. It means you need to identify any changes and choose which ones you can make. An adult curriculum, for example, that includes role play and bannermaking, will be used with difficulty by a class that has been used to sitting in rows for a lecture every week for the last forty years. It will be more comfortably used in a class that has tried some "active" learning, but has never used these specific learning activities.

Now, flip through other lessons to see if a variety of activities is suggested. Are activities repetitious? For example, a children's curriculum might suggest coloring preprinted pictures every lesson. Such repetition gets boring for both student and teacher. An appealing variety of learning activities is essential for children's classes. Some adult classes are less demanding in this matter.

Finally, in small churches we must be aware of expected class size. A study built around producing a play that requires ten actors is doomed to failure in a class of six.

Next, look at the lessons from the teachers' point of view.

- ★ Are instructions to the teachers clear and easy to follow?
- ★ Some curricula assume college-educated teachers who are willing and able to read a significant amount of complicated material to prepare for class. If you do not have such teachers, choose something else.
- ★ Some curricula offer only sketchy suggestions and expect teachers to develop specific plans. On the other hand, a curriculum may be *so* specific that it discourages individuality and creativity on the part of teachers. You need to identify materials between these extremes that are appropriate to your situation.
- ★ Is everything needed for the lesson provided in the material, or will the teacher have to find maps, commentaries, or unusual supplies?
- ★ How long do you think it would take to prepare each lesson?

Finally, consider the course from the student's point of view. If it includes material for students to read, is it appropriate to the reading level of the students? Be especially careful of this with children. Refer to the chapter on broadly graded classes for more details on appropriate reading materials for such classes. Does the course require outside preparation by students? If outside work is essential, and students (whatever their age) simply will not do it, select something else.

TEST #3—ATTRACTIVENESS: Some materials invite us to use them. Their color, arrangement, and form draw us to them. In this day of slick advertising, colorful books, and mass media, we are all very responsive to what a curriculum looks like. The most exciting message may go unheard if it is not presented in an interesting fashion—so evaluate the attractiveness of the curriculum.

Think particularly about its attractiveness to its intended users. Print size is important, especially to older adults and young children. Many teen-agers are looking for materials that do not remind them of school texts. Art work can draw people into, or repel them from, the curriculum.

THE THREE TESTS TOGETHER: When you have considered all three criteria separately (the message, teaching suggestions, and attractiveness), consider them together. Few curricula will pass all three tests with flying colors. Rather, they will excel in some areas more than others. At this point, your own judgment of the materials and knowledge of your local situation must meet and form the basis of your decision.

Any material that offers an unacceptable message must be discarded, no matter how teachable or attractive it is. As a general rule, it is more important for material to pass the message test and be teachable than it is for it to be attractive. But there are exceptions. One class found a curriculum whose message and teaching methods they were truly excited about. They did not use it, however, because the print of the study book was unreadable by the majority of the students, most of whom were over sixty and had cataract problems. In another example, an attractive curriculum with a solid message, but limited suggestions for teaching activities, could be quite effective if used by an especially creative teacher. You are the ones to make these kinds of decisions.

The Process for Selecting a Curriculum

This all sounds like a lot of work. It is. But it need not be overwhelming. Your work can be streamlined and carried out as follows.

STEP ONE: Using the sources for materials you identified at the beginning of this chapter, gather all the materials you wish to consider. One or two people will have to take responsibility for borrowing or ordering these materials for review, or for setting up any necessary appointments at the resource center.

STEP TWO: Once you have gathered all the curricula to be considered for either one class or the church school as a whole, assign each set of materials to an individual or a pair for evaluation by the tests outlined in the preceding section.

STEP THREE: As a group, hear the evaluation of each individual or pair. On the basis of these reports, the group selects the curriculum they feel is most appropriate to their particular situation.

Steps two and three can be carried out in a single meeting. Begin the meeting by assigning the sets of materials to be evaluated. Then allow time for individuals or pairs to evaluate their particular materials. People may want to work on this in different corners of the building. After this step is completed, regather to share findings and make final selections, as in step three.

You may, however, prefer to assign step two work to be done before a meeting for step three work. Again, choose the way that is right for you.

Choosing a Curriculum for the Long Haul

The one matter left to be considered is the question of continuity. If people are to grow in their faith, they need to explore and be challenged by all parts of it over the years. This is particularly obvious with children. As they grow up, we want them to hear all the stories from the Bible, not just a few favorites. We want them to learn the meaning of our worship, to understand how the church works, to know the story of the church, and to struggle with how we live out our faith in everyday situations. We think this is necessary for their spiritual growth, and it is. But it is just as necessary for adults to continue their growth in all these areas. The adult class that only studies the Bible (and mainly the New Testament) is growing lopsided.

<table>
<tr><th>Year</th><th>*Old Testament</th><th>*New Testament</th><th>*The Church</th><th>*The Christian Life</th></tr>
<tr><td>'77-'78</td><td>Exile</td><td>Revelation</td><td>Worship
Theology 101</td><td>Prayer
World Missions Today</td></tr>
<tr><td rowspan="2">'79-'80</td><td colspan="2">How the Bible Came to Be</td><td rowspan="2">Reformation
Seasons and Sanctuary
Mission in the Caribbean</td><td rowspan="2">Christian Marriage</td></tr>
<tr><td>Pentateuch</td><td>Holy Week</td></tr>
<tr><td>'78-'79</td><td>Job</td><td>Paul's Growing Faith</td><td>American Church History
Understanding the Islamic Faith</td><td>Christians on Radio and TV
Witnessing
Death</td></tr>
</table>

*See guideline areas of study on page 46.

To be sure that classes are exploring all of the faith over the years, it is important to have an overall plan for the curriculum. There are three ways to pursue such a plan.

(1) TOTAL-CHURCH CURRICULUM: Select a curriculum that includes its own long-range plan for the entire church school, and require that all classes follow it. Most denominational, and many independent, curricula are "total-church curricula." Most of them are built on a carefully constructed overall plan. Explanations of these plans are easily available and should be carefully evaluated by a church considering adopting such a curriculum.

Such a total-church curriculum is a simple way to provide carefully selected materials that follow an overall plan. Once the curriculum is selected, the question of what you will study is settled, except for occasional evaluation to be sure it is still appropriate.

But such an approach also offers some disadvantages, in that any total-church curriculum inevitably has weak spots. One age level (for instance, youth) may generally be of poorer quality than the rest. If the overall plan is to be protected, the weak spots must be accepted and endured. Another drawback is lack of freedom to take advantage of exceptional opportunities outside the curriculum. A particularly good youth series from somewhere else, for example, may have to be passed up to protect the flow of the total-church curriculum. Nevertheless, in spite of these disadvantages, a total-church curriculum still is often the most effective approach to curriculum selection in small churches.

One total-church curriculum that tries to avoid such disadvantages by providing more local choice, is Christian Education: Shared Approaches (CE:SA). This curriculum is really a system of four curricula that was created by twelve Protestant denominations in partnership. Each of the four approaches explores our faith from a slightly different angle. Local churches are encouraged to choose the one of the four that is most appropriate to them, *or* to create their own total-church curriculum by combining selected portions of some or all of the four curricula.

Three planning processes are offered to help churches design their own total-church curriculum. The processes differ in the way they tackle evaluating local needs and interests, and in their complexity. The simplest requires twelve to fifteen hours of work by five or six people. The most complicated requires twelve to fifteen people working over a period of seven to twelve months. Many of the sponsoring denominations have staff people trained to help local churches decide which planning process to use, and even to lead them through one of the processes. If such staff people are available to you, their services could be invaluable.

There are many useful materials in these four curricula, offering the possibility of building a solid total-church curriculum that is tailor-made by a particular congregation for itself. In my opinion, however, none of the three planning processes is very useful in small churches, especially rural small churches. Instead of using them, I would suggest that small-church people study the explanations of each of the four approaches to select the one or ones that are most appropriate to them. You should then evaluate your chosen materials, using the tests described in this chapter, to make your final selection. Based on these evaluations, you can build your own total-church curriculum.

(2) CAFETERIA CURRICULUM: You may, however, decide that you need more spontaneity than a total-church curriculum (even a tailor-made total-church curriculum) allows. Some classes, especially adult classes, may want more freedom to study what is of current concern or interest. In this case, curriculum selection can become a yearly or even quarterly process. Classes approach all available study resources like a diner approaching a cafeteria line. They want to see what is there and choose accordingly.

Adult students in a class will often take responsibility for finding out what is available to them, evaluating it, and submitting it to the responsible group for approval. In such situations, the group responsible for curriculum selection needs to keep an eye on the long-range picture. For starters, they need to keep and refer to records of what has been studied. This can be done on a simple chart, as illustrated here.

Another step is to set up some guidelines to insure that students explore the totality of the faith. For instance, one small church insists that classes study some from the Old Testament and some from the New Testament each year. They also require that the curriculum offer balanced amounts of (1) Bible study, (2) study of the church's doctrines and work, and (3) study of issues relating our faith to our everyday lives. They preserve their guidelines in a wheel similar to the familiar balanced-diet wheels of nutrition.

(3) DO-IT-YOURSELF CURRICULUM: One final curriculum possibility, that is not as way-out as it may at

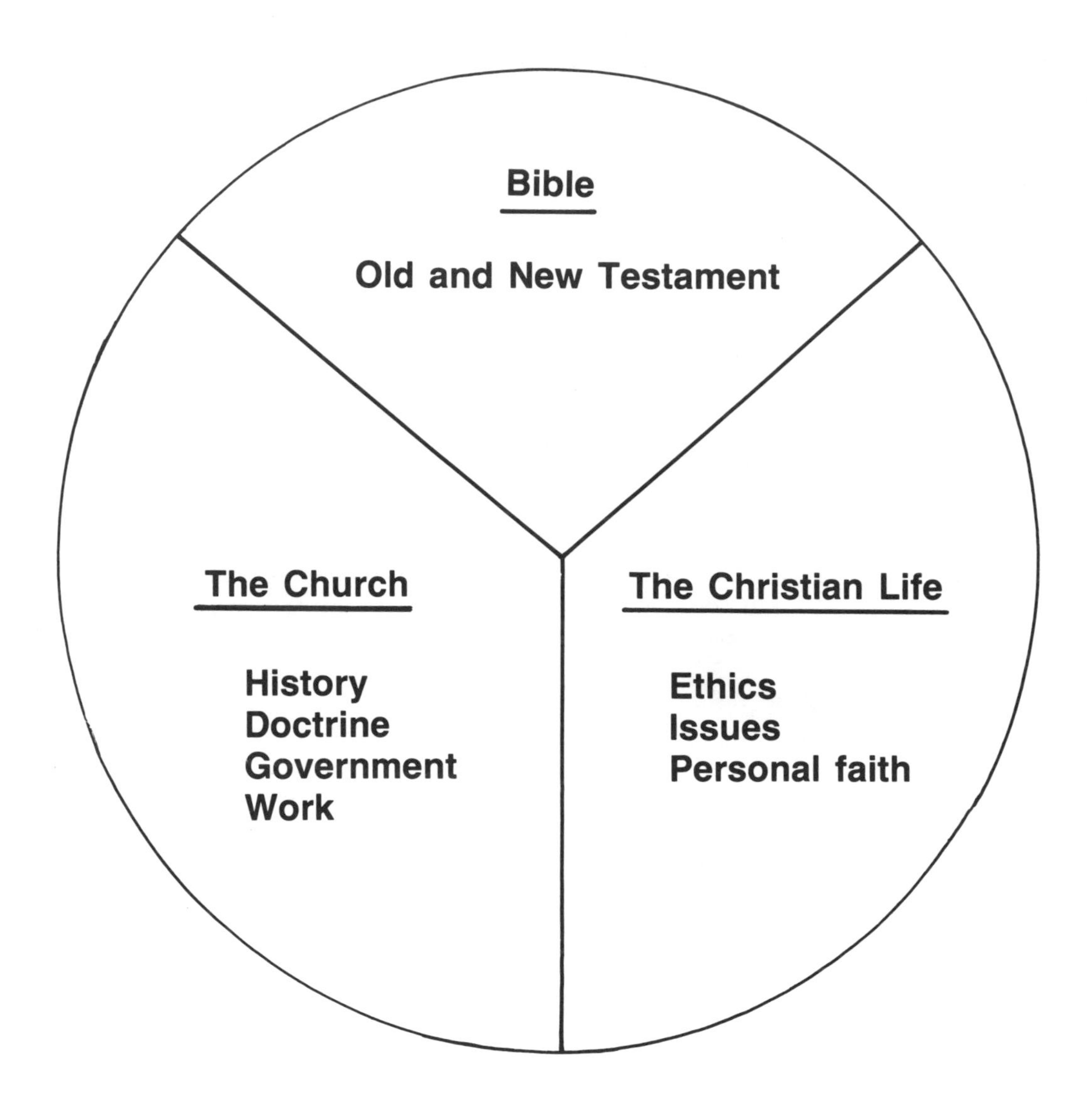

first seem, is to develop your own curriculum. The planning group develops guidelines and keeps records of the long-range situation, as in the cafeteria approach above. But instead of beginning by identifying what resources are available, they begin by identifying the subjects *they themselves* want and need to study. After identifying those subjects, they gather the materials needed to explore those subjects in the ways they want. This gives the local church maximum freedom in setting its own educational directions. Local church people decide what they will study, when they will study it, and how they will do it.

It is not as difficult as it sounds. Once the group has identified what it wants to study, all that is needed is two or three people who are aware of available resources and have the creativity to rearrange them to suit local needs. Several churches are proving this both possible and viable.

To prove to yourselves that you can do this, begin with a short-term event. Develop your own curriculum for Bible school or a Lenten study series.

Six:

How to Recruit Teachers

The very first obstacle to overcome in recruiting teachers is the feeling of hopelessness with which we tend to approach the job. Every recruiter in every church is sure that this will be the year when we really will not be able to find even the bare minimum number of teachers. In small churches, people claim the situation is the most difficult because of the small numbers they have to choose from. Large-church recruiters rightfully reply that their situation is equally tough because, though they have a larger group to recruit from, they must find a proportionately larger number of teachers to staff their classes. This sense of hopelessness can become a cloud that makes our requests to teach sound like invitations to doom.

So our first task as recruiters is to remind ourselves what it is we are doing. Recruiters are asking people to share their faith with other Christians. Teaching is a calling ranked high among the spiritual callings by Saint Paul. To be asked to teach is an honor, as well as a challenge. These teachers are going to be given carefully prepared and selected materials to work with and will have the support of the entire church. All of this is being done because the church places a very high value on Christian growth. So, set aside the cloud of doom, and approach the task of recruiting teachers for the church's education ministry with the prayerful energy it deserves.

Once you have gotten your task into the proper perspective plan your recruiting job by answering the following questions:

Question #1: Whom Will We Ask to Teach?

To answer this question, make yourself a big chart like the one illustrated. Down the left side of the page, list all the officers you must recruit and all the classes for which you must provide teachers. Be sure to include every office and every class, even those you are sure are already filled.

In a second column, list what each class will be studying during the coming year. Instead of listing the curriculum, list specific topics. For example, do not list International Sunday School Lessons for the adult class, but the topics for each quarter: the prophets, church history, Romans, and Genesis. These topics might influence your selection of teachers, and will surely influence the decisions of those you ask to teach.

Some classes do not have a curriculum. In such cases, make any notes about the content of those classes that might affect leader selection. The worship hour nursery, for example, may simply be child care. Note it as such.

Now you are ready for the crucial step. In the third column, make notes about the kind of leadership you want for each situation.

In the case of the officers, look at the list of jobs you have delegated to each position (see chapter 2) and briefly note the jobs you consider the most important this year. If the superintendent is to order the curriculum, lead opening assembly, and give moral support to teachers—but this year you want a superintendent who will concentrate on adding life to the opening assembly—list the three tasks, but star the important one. Be thoughtful here. Describe as clearly as possible what you are looking for.

In describing the teachers needed for each class, be as open to new possibilities as you can. Do not let what you have done in the past describe the future unless you want it to. There are many, many ways of providing teachers. Here are a few.

One Teacher and a Substitute

One person takes responsibility for teaching a class for one year. A dependable substitute is available to replace the teacher during sickness or vacation times.

Two- or Three-Person Teaching Team

Several people agree to teach a class together for a year. They plan together and are all on duty Sunday, sharing in the teaching of their class. Some teams of three plan their work so that each team member has one Sunday a month off. In small churches, we often think teaching teams are useful only in children's classes. However, teams are often welcomed in youth and adult classes as well, since two teachers pass leadership of

	CURRICULUM	LEADERS NEEDED	POSSIBILITIES	WHO ASKS
SUPERINTENDENT		record keeping * opening assembly	1. John Thomas 2. Jean Moore	Art
SECRETARY-TREASURER		collect money and deposit	Mr. T.	Art
ADULT CLASS	prophets church history Romans	different teacher for each topic-get teachers from that class	2. Madge, 1. Joan—Prophets Lathams—history 2. Martha, 1. Lou, or 3. Allen —Romans	Marge
YOUTH CLASS	survey of the Bible	a regular teacher dependable substitute	1. Kathy Ames 2. Janet Nicks	David - Kathy Marge - Janet
YOUTH FELLOWSHIP	they decide: learn by doing, not studying	2 couples	Browns Ellises Popes ask first Youngs	David
CHILDREN'S CLASS	Old Testament heroes, the disciples of Jesus	team of 2 plus 1 dependable substitute who will be extra helper when needed	Barry Kimes Kit Johns Ann Marie Pane sub = Jayne A.	Art - Kit, Barry Marge - Ann Marie
WORSHIP NURSERY	child care	a coordinator of week-by-week volunteers	Miss Jessica	David

the class back and forth and support each other during a session. Many people who would hesitate to teach alone will agree to be part of a team. Therefore, it is sometimes easier to recruit a team of two than to recruit one solo teacher.

Short-Term Teachers

Many people today cannot or will not commit themselves to long-term teaching jobs. The farmer has seasons during which there is time for nothing but farming. The college student is only home during the summer. The family of campers may be gone every summer weekend. Such people may be glad to accept short-term assignments that fit their schedules. To some, like college students, such a request may make them feel they are still an important part of their church. Classes often enjoy studying with different teachers because it offers variety. Therefore, you may want to recruit a different teacher for each unit or quarter a class will study in a year.

Topic Teachers

Everyone has some favorite topics or an area of special interest and even expertise. One way to provide a class with teachers is to recruit a teacher or team of teachers for each topic to be studied in a given year. Match people with their interests. If there is a unit on John, ask someone whose favorite Gospel is John to teach it. If the subject is church history, recruit someone who loves historical novels or has been on a tour of historical sites of the period to be studied. People who would say "no" to a general request might consider a short-term opportunity in their specialty.

Rotating Teachers

Some people prefer to teach alone but do not want to be tied down to "every Sunday." A pair of such teachers may happily share responsibility for one class. They may alternate months or units. Or, they may just agree which weeks each one will take. I suggest this approach hesitantly because its success depends on the attitude with which it is used. If both teachers are truly committed to the job and their students, it works fine. But if this is a desperation solution in which teaching is being done in the least demanding way possible, students (of any age) will recognize it for what it is. They will feel uncared for. Consequently, their enthusiasm for the class and their teachers will drop significantly. So consider this approach honestly.

Student-Teachers

The old adage is that the teachers learn more than the students. Some high school students can learn a great deal by teaching children for a period. This may simply mean that you consider occasionally recruiting a student to teach in any of the other patterns mentioned, or it may mean a carefully planned pattern in which several high school students teach together. In a very small church, the entire youth class might become the teachers of the children's class for a quarter or a year. In such a situation, the youths meet regularly (possibly monthly) with an adult helper to prepare for teaching. In these planning sessions, the adult leads them in studying on their own level what they will teach and then helps them plan their lessons. The adult does not attend the class they teach, except to help on a project at the student-teachers' request or to observe occasionally. High school student-teachers report that they have learned more than they did as students, that they enjoyed the job, and that they were pleased that their church trusted them to do it. The children enjoyed having youthful teachers and learned eagerly under their leadership.

Consider each class and its agenda for the coming year to provide teachers uniquely appropriate to it.

At this point, you need to list any qualifications for teachers that will affect your work. Some churches require that all teachers be members in good standing of their congregation. If you have any such requirements, make a note of them.

Only now are you ready to do the job we often start with—listing names of possible teachers. Actually, you may have already started your list as you described what you were looking for and thought of people who would be perfect for the job. That is fine, because the trick to recruiting teachers is matching the right person with the right job. As you do this, keep a few things in mind.

(1) *Look for surprises.* It is easy to get into the habit of asking or not asking certain people to do certain jobs. People who might be interested in teaching never get a chance because they are never asked. Frequently, when I begin working in a new church I accidently involve someone in something they have never done before. Everyone is very surprised because they have never thought of the person in that way. So look for surprises in people. Just because they have never done it, does not mean they would not give it a try and do well.

(2) *Beware of stereotypes.* (This is really a different version of #1.) Teachers come in both sexes, all ages, all levels of "educatedness," all shapes, and all persuasions. Be open to them. Men can teach children. Elderly people can be appreciated as wise teachers by teen-agers. Teen-age boys can be hero-teachers of children. Young adults can teach older adults. College-educated adults can enjoy and value the wisdom of a self-educated teacher. And, oh yes, middle-aged female homemakers can teach, too. So, do not be trapped by stereotypes. Be aware of and cultivate every potential teacher in your congregation. You need them ALL.

(3) *Match the person and the job.* This seems too obvious to state. However, we often "promote" excellent teachers to superintendent. In so doing, we lose a good teacher and do not necessarily gain a good superintendent. There are also many people who do excellent jobs as superintendents but will never be even passable teachers. Be aware of both the person and what you want done.

(4) *Cultivate a sense of responsibility for the children of your church.* Everyone agrees that it is better for parents not to teach their own children. Yet it often seems that they are the only ones willing to accept the job. Older adults say they took their turn when they were younger. Younger adults want to be in class, because they do not feel competent to teach yet, or because they are too busy. There is truth in their claims, but. . . . If this impasse is to be resolved, all members of the congregation are going to have to accept and act on their responsibility to children. In infant baptism, congregations pledge themselves to this responsibility. In the Presbyterian sacrament, all church members, not just the infant's parents, specifically promise to raise the child in "the nurture and admonition of the Lord." That includes teaching church school. Denominations that do not practice infant baptism profess responsibility of the congregation to raise its children to the age of decision. Remind people of that gently, throughout the year. Ask the minister to cultivate that understanding in the celebrating of the sacrament and in preaching. This project is a long-term investment but returns important dividends.

After you have completed your list of potential teachers, decide who will approach each one. Write their names in the last column, so that everyone knows for sure who is asking whom to do what.

Use the chart as a working record of your recruiting. As potential teachers are contacted, indicate their response. Add names to the "potential teacher" column as needed. This list insures that people are asked only once each year to teach. It can also provide a record to be referred to from one year to the next.

Question #2: When Will We Ask Them to Teach?

There is only one correct answer to this question: "Early!" Teachers should be recruited months before they are to teach. Because most church schools start their new year in September, teachers should be recruited in the spring.

There are several very practical reasons for this. First of all, we are not the only people out asking for commitments. The Scouts, United Way, civic clubs, political parties, country clubs, and public schools are all looking for volunteer leadership. If we wait until the last minute, we will find people already committed to other responsibilities. Even within the church there is competition for people to take responsible positions. If the women's organization, the men's organization, and the church board have secured their leadership before the church starts looking for teachers, many potential teachers will no longer be available. Bluntly put, it is the early bird that gets the worm.

Another reason for recruiting so far ahead is that you offer time for training and preparation. Many denominations offer summer training programs for church-school teachers. A teacher recruited in the spring has the option of taking one of these courses. Furthermore, teachers can begin gathering resources and ideas during the months before they start teaching. The time of preparation and training will produce better teaching.

Finally, recruiting done early lacks the feeling of panic and desperation that last minute recruiting has. We are able to pursue the job calmly and with poise. This affects both our feelings about the task, and the response of those we ask to teach. The whole job has more dignity and is more in the spirit of our education ministry. So recruit early.

Question #3: What Will We Ask Them to Do?

We all know stories about teachers who were promised that "it [teaching] won't take much time" or were told "there's nothing to it." In small churches, we know people fear that if they take any job, they may well have a lifetime assignment. We also know people who said they would be "helpers" and found themselves being "teachers." All of these situations make it difficult to recruit teachers. All of them can be easily avoided, if we will be as specific as possible about what we are asking people to do.

One way to be specific is to draw up a covenant or contract for teachers. In the contract, list exactly what the church expects of teachers and what it promises teachers. Give potential teachers copies of the contract and discuss it with them. Read the contract in worship the first Sunday of the church-school year. All of this clarifies what a church asks of teachers. When the job is clearly defined in this way, it is easier for people to evaluate their willingness to become teachers. It is also easier for them to say "yes." Designing a covenant is a simple three-step process.

STEP ONE: List the church's expectations of teachers. Include even the most obvious ones. If you expect teachers to be on time, say so, and set the time. If you expect them to be there or have a substitute there every Sunday, say so. (Some teachers would not worry if their class occasionally went a Sunday without a teacher. If this is unacceptable, be sure this is known from the beginning.)

If you expect teachers to follow a specific curriculum or implement given church policies, put it on the list.

Check your list of job assignments from chapter 2. Any jobs you assigned to teachers there, add to your list.

Sample List

We expect teachers to . . .

—plan carefully (2 hours/week—guideline)
—be in room by 9:50 to greet students and begin class at 10:00 SHARP
—use approved curriculum
—notify superintendent *EARLY* when a substitute is needed
—attend worship
—attend training workshops
—pray for students

STEP TWO: Now list what the church promises its teachers. Include resources and services that will be provided to help teachers do their job. Look at the task assignments made in chapter 2 to identify the support teachers can expect from other church-school officers. (If this step is harder than step one, read the chapter on the care and feeding of small-church teachers to finish the list.)

Sample List

The church will . . .

—provide curriculum and basic resources required in curriculum
—provide substitutes (through superintendent)
—provide basic A-V equipment and someone to operate it (when needed)
—pay fees and travel costs for training workshops
—support your work through Education Committee
—pray for you and your work

STEP THREE: Type the lists on one page. Make copies for all potential teachers.

SAMPLE COVENANT

Teaching is a high calling, a ministry. It is both demanding and rewarding. Those who accept a call to this ministry should do so fully aware of what they are undertaking and the support they can expect from the church that calls them.

The Cross Roads Church expects teachers to:

> *(1) Make careful preparations and plans for your class each week, following the suggested plans in the provided curriculum. Two hours of preparation for a week's lesson seems to be a good guideline.*
> *(2) Prove the church's concern for your students by regular attendance. Contact the superintendent* at least one week in advance *when possible, when you need a substitute.*
> *(3) Be* prompt. *Though church school officially starts at 10:00* A.M., *we encourage you to get to your room five to ten minutes early to welcome early students and be prepared to begin your lesson at 10:00* A.M. *sharp. This time of visiting and settling in before class can be a most valuable part of your session.*
> *(4) Keep your own faith growing, and set an example for your students by regular attendance at worship.*
> *(5) Attend appropriate workshops and teachers' meetings to improve your skills.*
> *(6) Love and pray for your students.*

Teachers can expect the church to:

> *(1) Give you strong administrative support through the church-school superintendent and the Christian Education committee.*
> *(2) Provide carefully selected curriculum and resources for you to use in your class. If you need help in using the curriculum, or feel a need to change materials, contact the superintendent.*
> *(3) Make substitutes available. We do not want you to feel guilty when you need to be away from church on Sunday. We want to take care of you by taking care of your class when you are sick.*
> *(4) Provide a record player, cassette recorder, and filmstrip projector with an operator, if needed. We will help locate and borrow any other equipment you need. Ask the superintendent for equipment.*
> *(5) Pay registration fees and travel expenses for any teacher training workshops you attend. We will also help arrange for and pay for child care to enable you to attend workshops.*
> *(6) Love you and pray for you and your work.*

Specifically we are asking you to: team teach the youth class with Agnes Jones from September 1980 through August 1981.

Such a contract clearly outlines what you are asking a teacher to do. To some people it may seem a bit cold and businesslike for a church to issue contracts. They would prefer more informal, personal "understandings." Unfortunately, such understandings are never as clear as we later wish. So I would suggest that you use the written contract/covenant. One way to personalize the agreement is to use the word "covenant" instead of "contract." "Covenant" carries religious meanings of holy commitments that, in many churches, would remove the cold, businesslike feeling of "contract."

Question #4: How Will We Ask Them?

The way we ask our question says something about what we think about the importance of the question. You may quickly ask several people to bring cookies for a reception while they are visiting with each other on the sidewalk after church. But a young man may take hours setting the scene to ask his girlfriend to marry him. In fact, if he did not go to some trouble to ask the question in an important way, his girl may think he equates marriage with such mundane things as reception cookies, and answer accordingly. Therefore, the way we ask people to teach should communicate something of the importance we attach to the job.

Instead of asking people "when we see them around church" or calling them on the phone to pose our question, we need to arrange a time when we can talk with each potential teacher uninterruptedly for at least fifteen minutes. In most cases, this requires a visit in their home. Call ahead to arrange a convenient time. It is best, if possible, to avoid stating the purpose of your visit. Simply say that you need to talk to them for a few minutes. This avoids allowing them to make their decision before you get to present your request fully. People may guess why you are coming and have some tentative excuses or interests in mind, but they are more open to hear the request.

During the visit, you need to:

(1) discuss the proposed covenant

(2) show the curriculum to be used
(3) list the students, and
(4) answer any questions the potential teacher has.

This is not the time to ask for a commitment. If the person is at all willing to consider your request, leave a copy of the covenant and the curriculum for them to examine more closely. Ask them to call you, or promise to call them in a week to get their answer.

Such a visit says you care about teaching and the people who teach. It says that being asked to teach is an honor. After all, some people have obviously given selecting teachers great thought and effort, which led to choosing THEM instead of someone else. And it says that if they teach, they had better plan to take the job as seriously as the church does. Such messages make this way of asking people to teach well worth the time.

Question #5: What If They Say No?

Be gracious. Accept their decision as one they have made after careful consideration. Do not twist arms. However, do try graciously to learn what led them to say no. It may be that they misunderstood some part of your request and would say yes to what you really wanted. It may be a matter of timing. They might be willing to teach next year after Janie starts school, or during the winter instead of the summer, when they like to be at the lake. It may be that you asked them to teach the wrong class. Teen-agers baffle them, but they would gladly take a turn teaching an adult class. Finally, it may be that they just do not want to teach. They would gladly do anything else—like fill one of the offices—but they do not want to teach. Any of this is very useful information. Note it on your working chart. Then follow up on it in the appropriate way at the appropriate time.

Question #6: Who Will Ask Them?

The job is too big for one person in all but the smallest of churches. The natural thing is for the "responsible group," which produced the covenant and identified the needs, to do the recruiting. Within that group, individuals may split up recruiting responsibilities in any way that suits them. One person may take responsibility for recruiting all the leadership for a given class. Or people may agree to speak to candidates to whom they feel they could most effectively state the request. In either case, keep in close touch with each other on your progress.

NOTE: In some denominations, teachers must be approved by the ruling board. Ask your minister what kind of approval is necessary in your church. Then, be sure to follow whatever procedures he or she outlines.

This chapter, with its six questions on recruiting, is quite long, and suggests more than a little work. But it is important work. It is important because it involves building foundations for, and basic attitudes of, the people who teach in our church schools. If you do your recruiting carefully and well, you are on the way to a successful church school.

Seven:

The Care and Feeding of the Small-Church Teacher

Great church-school teachers are not born. They develop and grow. The most mature, sensitive Christian adult does not automatically become a gifted teacher the moment he or she accepts the challenge to teach. Teachers are people who have learned the skills of story-telling, directing dramatic learning activities, planning lessons from less-than-perfect study books, keeping classroom discipline, asking the right question at the right time, and so forth. Church-school teachers are farmers and lawyers and housewives who have agreed to spend several hours of their precious free time each week to be the best possible teachers under less-than-ideal circumstances. Such people are very special, and therefore need and deserve special "care and feeding" so that they do indeed become the best possible teachers, and so that they get some personal satisfaction out of teaching.

Small-church teachers require three basic kinds of care and feeding to thrive. They need:

Encouragement. Teaching in a small church can be a very lonely job. Often teachers are given their books and then left to fend for themselves. In that situation, teachers may feel that they are trying to do a job that is more than they can handle, that they are spending too much time on it, and that no one cares about it anyway. All of this can be avoided if some people are keeping in touch with teachers. It is the little things that count here: student compliments reported to teachers, a phone call to ask how things are going, including teachers in the public prayers of the church from time to time, etc. Teachers need to know that their work is valued by the church and that the church supports them as they teach.

Skills. Teaching requires some very specific learnable skills. All teachers, for example, need to be able to ask questions that will help students explore ideas, and will check up on student knowledge. Teachers for different ages need different skills. Teachers of children need to know how to tell a story well, how to make painting a mural a learning experience instead of just busy work, and how to use puppets. Teachers of older students need some skills in leading group research, using case studies, creative Bible study methods, etc. The church needs to provide opportunities for teachers to acquire such skills.

Inspiration. People who volunteer to teach in church school usually view their work as teachers as a commitment to do God's work. This sense of commitment needs to be honored and developed. There is a great deal of emphasis in the Bible on teaching and teachers. We need to provide opportunities for teachers to read and reflect on these, so that they can grow in their understanding of what it means to be a teacher in the church of Jesus Christ. This understanding will increase both their effectiveness as teachers and the personal pleasure they find in their work.

There are many different ways a church can offer the encouragement, skill training, and inspiration that are necessary to teachers for their growth.

(1) Going Away to Workshops

Each year, districts, conferences, associations, presbyteries, and even denominations sponsor a vast variety of workshops for church-school teachers. They range in length from one day, to a weekend, to a full week. Generally, these workshops are led by people in your region or by well-known leaders in specific areas of Christian education. Most teachers find such workshops useful. They are the source of new ideas, and one way to polish teaching skills. But most teachers are slow to sign up for workshops.

That is where church-school superintendents and members of the responsible group come in. Someone needs to be aware of what is being offered and actively encourage teachers to attend those that apply to them. Most denominations send out information about upcoming workshops to all churches in the denomination. Find out who gets this mailing in your church. It is most likely the minister. If your minister is getting this information, work with him or her to plan a way to get it to the right people. Ministers are mailed an enormous amount of stuff. As a result, a lot of good, useful information gets lost in the piles on and around their desks. This is especially true if the minister's desk is away from your church building, either at home or in another church. One way to avoid this is to establish a place where the minister can drop all education mailings so that they can be picked up by people working in that ministry. Some ministers have to be prodded to keep up with this, so prod if necessary. This is vital information worth prodding to get.

Once you know what is available, evaluate its usefulness for each of your teachers. Do not encourage teachers to attend every workshop you hear about. Instead, select those that especially fit each teacher in that particular class situation. If teachers learn that you only suggest workshops that turn out to be worthwhile, they will be more responsive to your suggestions. Do not tell a brand new teacher, who is struggling with basics, about the great workshop on simulation gaming. Save it for the experienced teacher who is looking for something new to add life to the class. Do tell the new teacher about the "Introduction to Teaching Youth" workshop that promises to base its work on the very curriculum that this teacher is using.

It is also important to time your workshop offerings. A good workshop creates some enthusiasm that affects teaching for some time, but does not last forever. Therefore, it is often wise to spread out your suggestions. New teachers are usually ready for a workshop in the early fall. That, plus the excitement of Christmas activities, may carry them into the winter. Most teachers appreciate a good workshop in February or March. Those months are often the "longest" in the church-school year. Some fresh insights, ideas, and enthusiasm may be just what is needed to perk things up. Timing also means not suggesting too many workshops too close together. This can be frustrating when several "really great" opportunities come along at the same time. In this situation you must use careful judgment on which ones to "mention" and which ones to "encourage."

The difference in "mentioning" and "encouraging" a workshop is critical. Just telling teachers about workshops is not enough. Just posting the announcement of a workshop on the bulletin board is not enough. Both of these are not enough, because they only "mention" the existence of the workshops. You need to "encourage" teachers to attend. That means offering to have the church send in their registration fee, telling them who else is going, asking if you could keep their children during the event, and helping them get transportation when needed. It means calling a second time if someone said they would think about it. "Encouraging" takes time, but it gets results.

Often in the fall or spring there are training events that offer many different workshops at the same time and place. This is a good opportunity to get a carload of teachers off for training and the fun of going together. Even if you do not teach, go along. Take one of the courses. There is frequently one for superintendents or members of education committees. Share in the talk after the workshops. Often in the car on the way home "great plans" are made. Be part of this planning and dreaming session, and then help make the plans and dreams come true when you get home. Once you have "encouraged" one of these successful expeditions, it will be easier to get people to go along on the next one.

Many denominations offer week-long Christian education conferences during the summer at their national conference centers. These conferences offer a variety of teacher training courses and speakers on themes related to the education ministry of the church. The leadership is drawn from throughout the denomination and is usually quite good. Such conferences provide opportunities for in-depth training in teaching skills, inspiration from the speakers, and worship with a gathering of Christian teachers. Because these conference centers are often in resort areas and offer recreation bonuses, many people view a week at one of these conferences as a kind of vacation. Though it is often difficult to get teachers to go to one of these for the first time; once exposed to them, many teachers return. For some it is an annual pilgrimage. A group of teachers from one church (even a small one) may go every year and stay in the same cottage together. For such a group the conference is a source of training, inspiration, and fellowship that they value highly.

How to Get Started

(1) Find out what kinds of area workshops are available to your teachers by asking your minister and/or regional denomination staff person.

(2) Learn how such events are announced and publicized. Make plans to get this information to the appropriate teachers. (A) If your minister receives this informaton, make plans with him or her to get it to appropriate people. Consider a drop-off place, or create a system that will work for you. (B) You may want to assign someone to "encourage" attendance at appropriate workshops.

(2) Offering Workshops in Your Own Church

Workshops sponsored by districts of churches offer fine opportunities for teacher training. Unfortunately, a significant number of people will not travel more than about thirty minutes to get to a workshop. Night workshops in neighboring churches are equally hard to get people to attend. That means that the most effective teacher training may be done in your own church. Yet this is probably the most overlooked possibility in small churches, because most of us wrongly believe we do not have the leadership to do such things. This simply is not true.

The easist way to provide local training is to hold monthly or quarterly meetings for all teachers in your church. Each meeting will be part business and part training. Open the meeting with a devotional especially for teachers. Then, under the direction of the superintendent (or whoever is assigned the job), church-school business can be conducted. This is time for coordinating special projects and being sure every teacher understands the plans for the next church season and/or any new education programs and policies. Dreams can be shared and plans made to implement them. Needs can be identified and responded to. Teachers can share their successes and failures. Fifteen to thirty minutes spent in such business will yield a more smoothly running church school and can knit the teachers into a team that both supports, and feels supported by, the church. The final forty-five minutes of the meeting is reserved for teacher training. In each meeting, attention is focused on one skill or phase of teaching that is important to all the teachers of the church school. One meeting might focus on how to evaluate a session. In another, teachers might try out a lesson planning process or get experience in using a new study book (a concordance, for instance). Each meeting becomes a mini-workshop.

There are many resources for such local mini-workshops. Most denominations and several independent Christian educators have produced kits and books that help teachers teach themselves, or provide instructions for local teacher training sessions. Your denomination's catalog of church school materials will probably include a page or more of these resources. They cost no more than study materials we routinely provide for students. And, because they enable teachers to make more effective use of the materials we already purchase, they are well worth the additional investment. (They can also be reused. Start building a *small* library of them.)

Teaching Teachers to Teach, by Donald L. Griggs, is a good example of a useful resource. This is a "how-to" manual. Many chapters include worksheets that teachers can use alone or together as they acquire and polish teaching skills. Each of these chapters can become a mini-workshop of one or more sessions. For example, at their monthly meeting, one group of teachers and I worked through chapter 9, "The Art of Asking Questions." I presented part of the chapter as a lecture and then led in working through the exercises. The teachers taped one of their class sessions on a cassette recorder during the following month, and brought the tape to the next teachers' meeting. At that meeting, each teacher listened to his or her own tape with a worksheet made up from suggested questions in the book. That exercise has often been cited as one of their most useful training experiences by those teachers. All of the instructions came directly from *Teaching Teachers to Teach.* (Note: At the back of the book there are "Ten Descriptions of Teacher Education Events." These events would require resources beyond the book, and the work of a professional educator. My suggestion is that small-church teachers work through the first twelve chapters as outlined in the book. These chapters provide more than a year's supply of mini-workshops for teachers' meetings.)

Teaching Teachers to Teach is only one of many teacher training resources available from Don and Pat Griggs. These resources are available in religious bookstores and resource centers.

"This is all very interesting," you say. "But who is going to lead these training sessions?" None of the books and kits mentioned here require "expert" leadership. They include step-by-step instructions that enable any person with a little teaching background to lead others through the suggested learning activities. There are probably several people in your church who could be leaders for such sessions.

- ⋆ The most obvious one may be your minister—if he or she has some training and interest in Christian education. Many ministers find this an excellent way to be involved in the church school—especially if they cannot be present during the church school sessions on Sunday mornings.
- ⋆ If your minister is not so interested or trained, consider the public school teachers in your congregation. Many current teachers do not want to teach on Sunday morning after teaching all week, but would be willing to become the "teacher of teachers" for monthly or quarterly meetings. Do not overlook retired schoolteachers either. Many of them have excellent skills and the time to plan and lead workshops using the resources described above. A "teacher of teachers" could be recruited every year along with other teachers and officers.
- ⋆ A final possibility is to hire a professional Director or Minister of Education from a neighboring church to

lead regular training sessions at your church. If you do this, make a clear written contract stating what you expect of each other. Then honor it. Avoid the temptation to use them beyond the agreement.

In summary, while very few small churches consider the possibility of offering teacher training in their own church, resources that can be used by the kind of leaders of teachers found in most small churches are available to us. My experience with monthly teachers' meetings for business and training is that they are effective and produce warm, caring communities that teachers enjoy.

How to Start

(1) Find out what teacher training resources are offered in your denomination's catalog. Order one or two to preview.

(2) Borrow or buy a copy of *Teaching Teachers to Teach,* and plan a way to use it in your church.

(3) Discuss the possibilities of a monthly or quarterly teachers' business and training meeting in your church. What potential and problems do you see in it? Who would be your most likely teachers of teachers?

(3) Subscribing to Teachers' Magazines

One way teachers can improve their skills and insights, in the comfort of their own home, is reading teachers' magazines. These magazines include articles on specific skills, stories about teaching successes, reviews of new books and resources that might interest teachers, directions for making inexpensive classroom equipment, poetry, and inspirational reading for teachers. Teachers who make a habit of reading such a magazine claim to benefit from and enjoy it.

The only challenge about this, in a busy world, is finding time to do the reading. To get around this, some churches ask one person to review magazines in order to identify the articles that would be of interest to each teacher. If the church orders a copy for each teacher, the reviewer marks the articles in each teachers' copy. If the church buys one or two copies to share among teachers, the reviewer may cut the copies up, giving the teachers the articles that apply to their specific situations. The reviewer's hope is that a teacher who may not pick up a whole magazine will read a few articles picked out with him or her in mind.

There are several excellent teachers' magazines. Most denominations publish one designed especially for their teachers. Your denomination's church-school materials catalog will probably include the name and a description of any teachers' magazine for your denomination. Though these vary in quality, you would be wise to order at least a trial subscription to whatever magazine your denomination publishes.

There are also two national teachers' magazines worth trying. *Church Teachers,* published by the National Teacher Education Project, is a forty-page magazine published five times a year. Most of the articles in each issue are written by lay church-school teachers about things that have worked for them. Order it from: *Church Teachers* Magazine, 7214 East Granada Road, Scottsdale, Arizona 85257.

Share is published in a news magazine quarterly for the twelve Joint Education Development (JED) denominations. It includes a wide variety of articles on needs, programs, and concerns in all Christian denominations, as well as practical suggestions for seasonal emphases and listings of new resources. *Share* deals with education ministries in the broadest sense of the term, while *Church Teachers* deals almost exclusively with church school. Order *Share* from this address: JED *Share,* 132 W. 31 St., New York, N.Y. 10001.

How to Get Started

(1) Order sample copies of *Church Teachers, Share,* and your denomination's teacher magazine to evaluate for use in your church. You may want to ask the teachers to be part of the evaluation and selection.

(2) Once you have selected a magazine or magazines, plan how you will make it available to your teachers, and encourage them to read it.

(4) Dedicating Students and Teachers

Begin the church-school year with a dedication service that is worthy of the high calling of Christian education. A lot of work will have already gone into arranging classes, selecting curriculum, and recruiting teachers. A lot more work will go into planning lessons, supporting teachers, and learning together in classes. Therefore, it is important to everyone involved to set aside a time when all this work can be raised before each other and before God in worship.

There are as many ways to do this as there are congregations. Some churches make it a big party, with the dedication service taking place during a church supper or breakfast (the breakfast may be pancakes and sausage cooked by a group of volunteers, a covered dish feast, doughnuts and juice or coffee, or whatever is wished). Some churches simply have a special worship service during the church-school hour. Others plan the morning worship service around the theme of growing in faith. The sermon, music, and prayers are related to the theme and climax in a service of teacher and student dedication. Some churches recognize and thank all outgoing teachers and officers. Some give children certificates of promotion. Special gifts may be given. For example, children of a certain age may be given a Bible each year. Some churches work hard to invite everyone who may not be regular in attendance to be part of this day (and, they hope, to become more active in church school). Do whatever you do in your church to celebrate BIG events.

The heart of all these celebrations is the dedication of teachers and students. This involves some promises (in many ways it is like a wedding). Teachers promise God and their students to do their best possible job. Students promise God and their teachers that they will be diligent students. You will probably need to write these promises yourself. As you do, make them as specific as possible. Include such spiritual specifics as praying for each other, and such mundane specifics as getting to church school regularly and on time. The sample promises included were used in a morning worship service built around the theme of opening up to God's word and will. They reflect that theme. Your promises would be different to reflect your theme.

SAMPLE PROMISES

This morning we start a new church-school year. It is a time for teachers to be installed in their new responsibilities. It is a time for students to rededicate themselves to learning.

TEACHERS: So I ask teachers to stand where you are as I read your names (read names, etc.). And I ask you now: Do you promise before God and these brothers and sisters in Christ that you will open up space in your life to teach? Do you promise to set aside time to plan lessons, to gather supplies, to be at church school on time and prepared? Will you also promise to open yourself to love and to care for each one of your students? IF SO, ANSWER "I DO."

Do you further promise to open up yourself and your students to God's Word? Will you take care that what you share with your students is God's Word rather than your own ideas? Do you promise to challenge your students—even when they don't want the challenge—to open themselves to God's Word, to break out of their limited human understanding to hear God speaking? IF SO, ANSWER "I DO."

STUDENTS: And now I ask all students to stand. You have heard what your teachers have promised. Theirs is a nearly impossible job, but they have opened themselves to give it their best try.

Will you now promise God and promise them that you will open your hearts and lives to receive them as teachers? Specifically, will you come regularly and on time? Will you try out what they offer? Will you pray for them and take care of them? IF SO, ANSWER "I WILL."

Furthermore, do you promise to open yourself up to learning and growing in the faith? Will you attempt to hear God's Word—even when it doesn't agree with what you already think? And will you open your life to the changes called for as you grow? IF SO, ANSWER "I WILL."

LET US PRAY TOGETHER. Father, as we begin a new church-school year, we ask your blessings and your presence with all who teach of your Word, and to living it out everyday. Protect our promises. Remind us of them when we are tempted to give them less than our best; when we decide to wing it, rather than fully prepare our lesson; when we are about to sleep in on Sunday. In addition, we ask that you add your blessings to our promises and intentions so that our teaching will surpass our abilities and our learning will take us beyond our own ideas. Open us up, Father, even as you opened yourself up to us in your Son. For we make our promises in his name, AMEN.

If you are in the sanctuary or similar setting, teachers and students may stand in place to make their promises. If you have more space, classes of students may form circles around their teachers to make their promises.

Such a dedication service offers teachers a chance to formally commit themselves to the ministry of teaching. It may be a source of inspiration. It also give them a sense of the church's support for teachers and an idea of the value the church places on teaching. All of this is food for growing teachers.

How to Get Started

(1) Set a date and plan your celebration. Be sure to include the minister in your planning meeting if you hope to have the service of dedication during Sunday morning worship.

(2) Keep a copy of your plans and the promises to help you get started next year.

In addition to these major ways of caring for and feeding small-church teachers, there are many, many "little" things that mean a lot to teachers. The next pages are a gallery of them. There are others. . . .

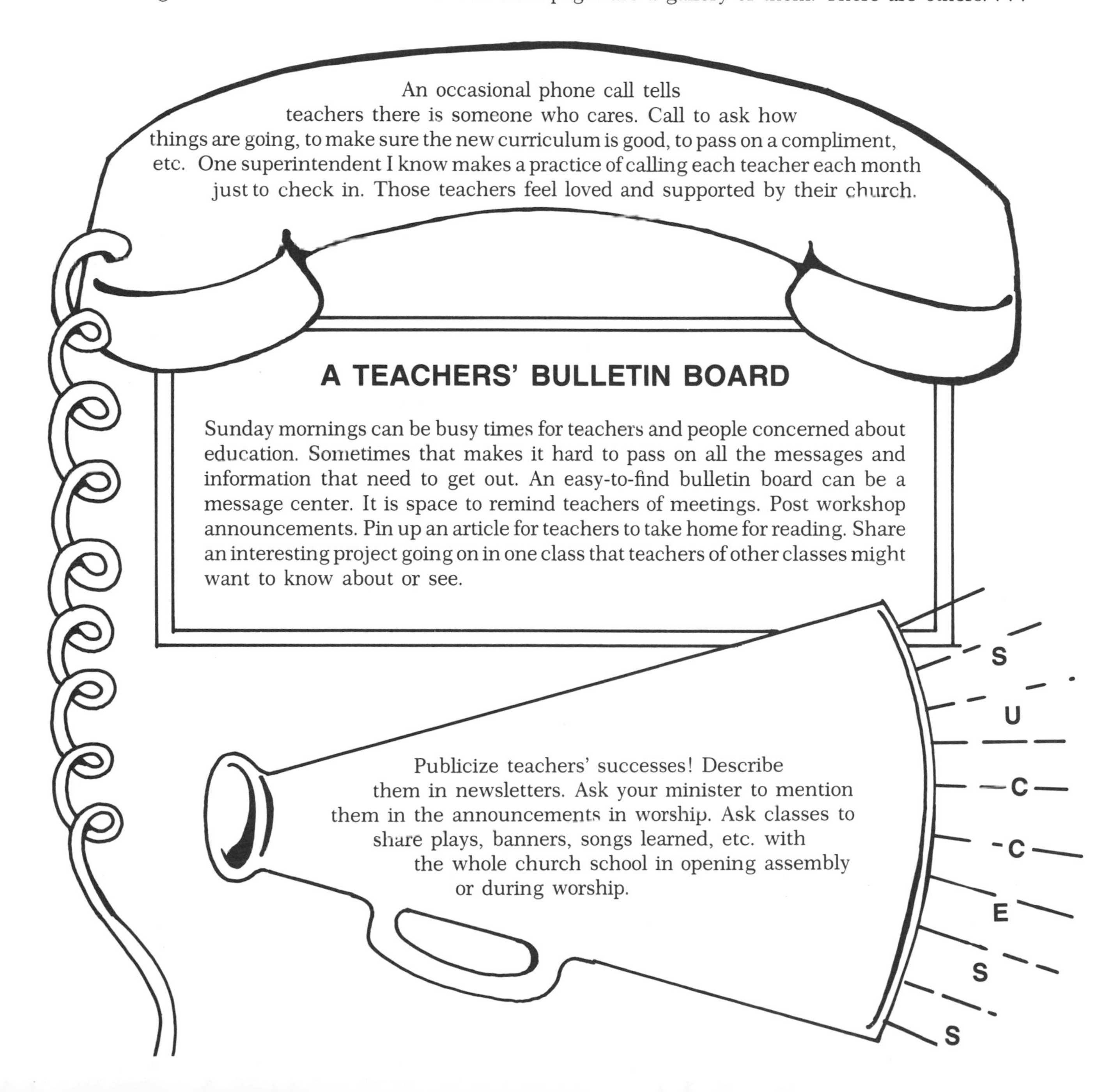

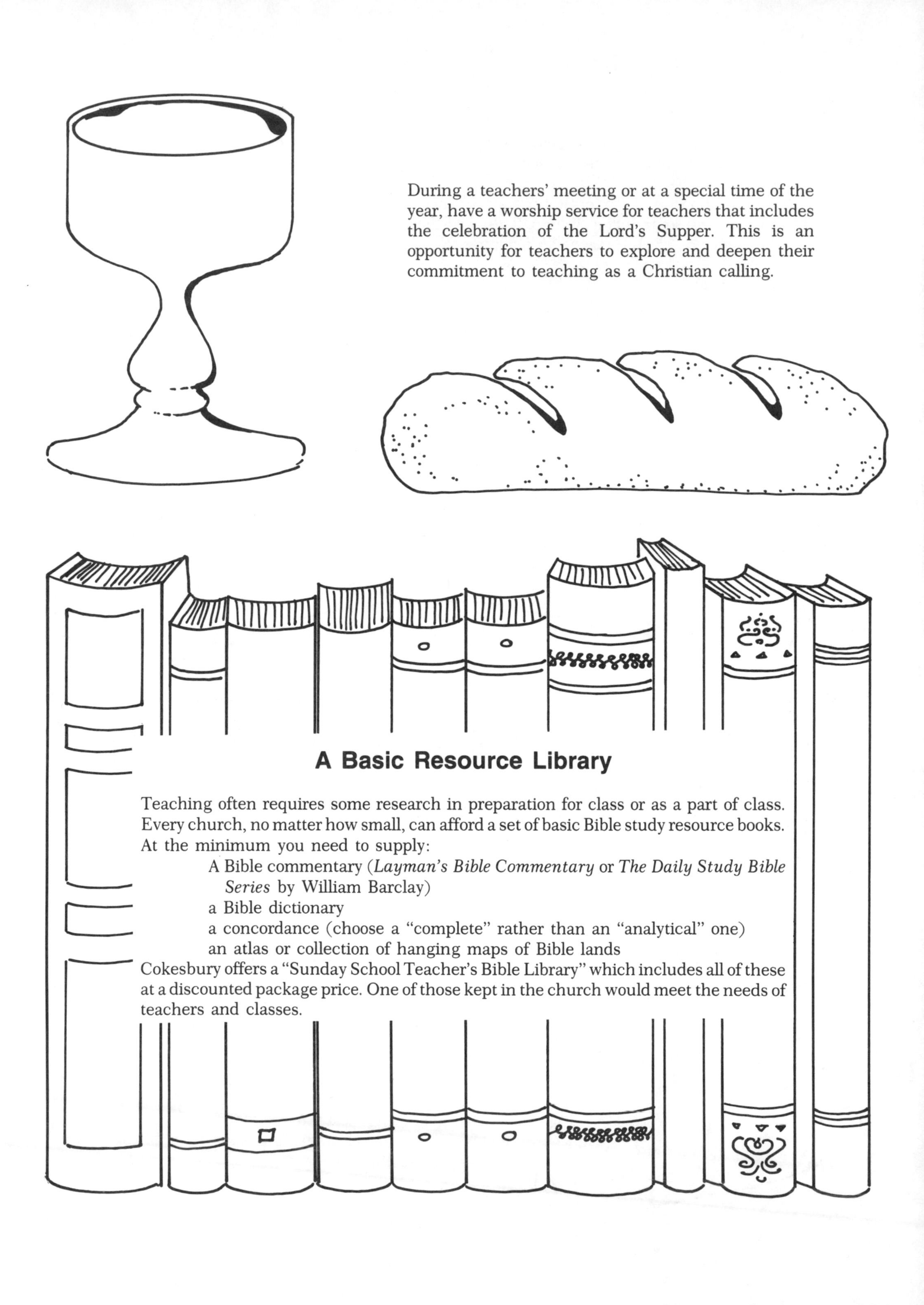

During a teachers' meeting or at a special time of the year, have a worship service for teachers that includes the celebration of the Lord's Supper. This is an opportunity for teachers to explore and deepen their commitment to teaching as a Christian calling.

A Basic Resource Library

Teaching often requires some research in preparation for class or as a part of class. Every church, no matter how small, can afford a set of basic Bible study resource books. At the minimum you need to supply:

A Bible commentary (*Layman's Bible Commentary* or *The Daily Study Bible Series* by William Barclay)
a Bible dictionary
a concordance (choose a "complete" rather than an "analytical" one)
an atlas or collection of hanging maps of Bible lands

Cokesbury offers a "Sunday School Teacher's Bible Library" which includes all of these at a discounted package price. One of those kept in the church would meet the needs of teachers and classes.

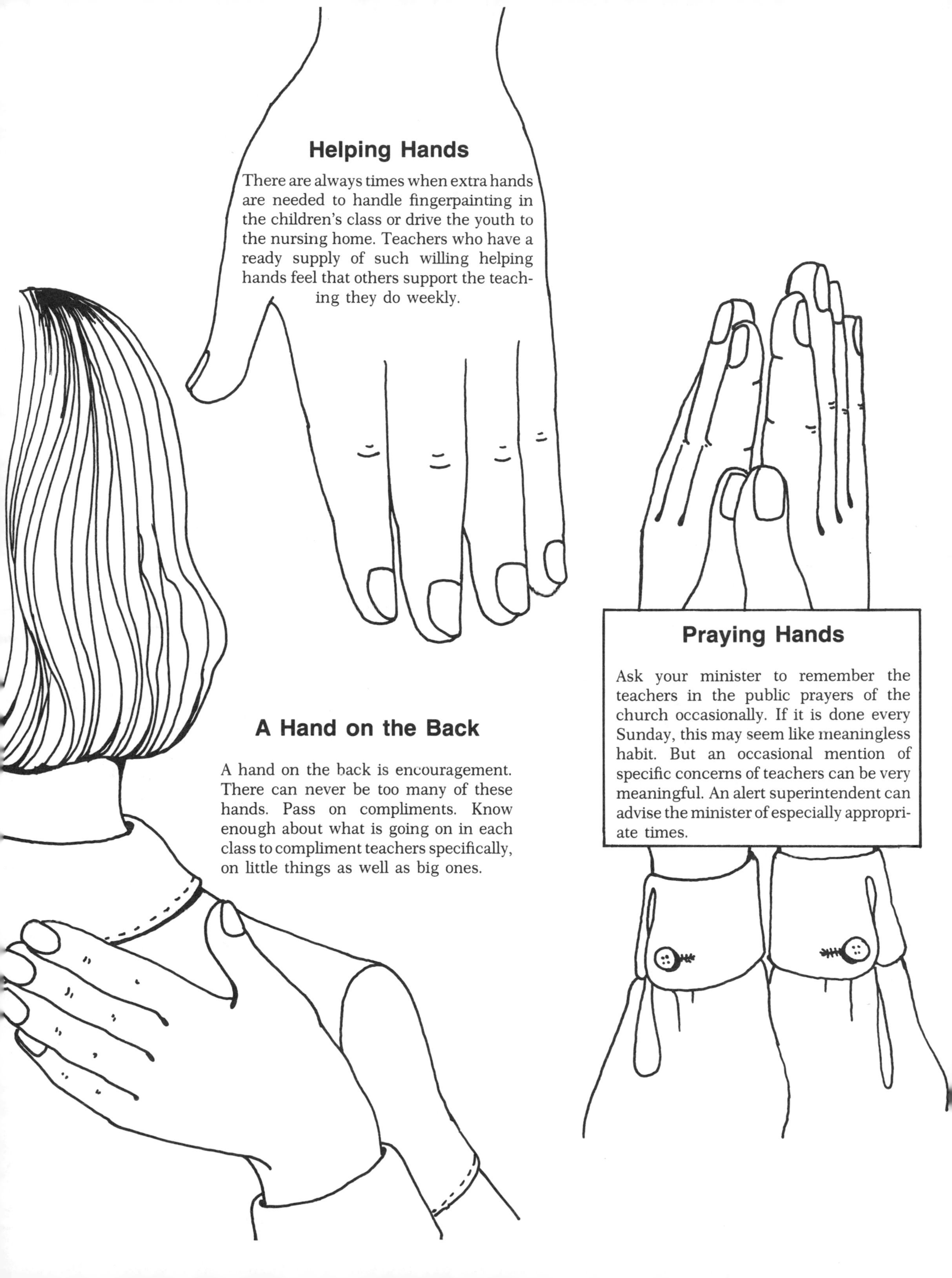
Helping Hands
There are always times when extra hands are needed to handle fingerpainting in the children's class or drive the youth to the nursing home. Teachers who have a ready supply of such willing helping hands feel that others support the teaching they do weekly.
A Hand on the Back
A hand on the back is encouragement. There can never be too many of these hands. Pass on compliments. Know enough about what is going on in each class to compliment teachers specifically, on little things as well as big ones.
Praying Hands
Ask your minister to remember the teachers in the public prayers of the church occasionally. If it is done every Sunday, this may seem like meaningless habit. But an occasional mention of specific concerns of teachers can be very meaningful. An alert superintendent can advise the minister of especially appropriate times.

A personal note is appreciated any time of the year. Write to thank a teacher for an especially good job or love beyond the call of duty. Send a card on their birthday or anniversary with no reference at all to teaching.

A valentine can say that you are loved for what you are doing as a teacher. Buy inexpensive "Teacher" valentines, or make old-fashioned valentines for each teacher. If you can do it on the sly, encourage students to make or send ♡'s to their teachers.

Gift-giving can get out of hand, but an occasional little gift can also make a person feel loved. One Christmas, a church sent each teacher a card with a Christian symbol lapel pin included. On the first Sunday of the church-school year, another church gives each teacher a book or resource that is particularly appropriate for them. Others give gifts at the end of term. The most appreciated gifts are those that are unexpected or those that are obviously picked out with only one person in mind. Plan teacher gifts accordingly.

At the end of the year, show the church's appreciation for the teacher's work by throwing a party for them.

The party may be a picnic or dinner in the home of a non-teaching church member. One church goes to a Chinese restaurant and orders a dinner for thirteen and enjoys tasting and passing around all the dishes. If a responsible group has been supporting the teachers, they may want to provide the dinner or go along paying their own way, while the church pays for the teachers. The more of a team the teachers have been during the year, the more they will enjoy an end of the year party.

Pin a flower on each teacher on their last day of teaching, and publicly thank them for their work. These do not have to be store-bought corsages. A pretty garden flower says it all.

At the end of the teachers' term, one church gives each teacher a book selected especially for them and signed by the members of their class. The book may be a story tool, a devotion book, a book related to the topic they taught or their special interest, or anything else that seems appropriate for that particular teacher.

at the end of their term

Assignment

This chapter included eighteen ways to support and train teachers in small churches. Every church is not going to use every suggestion. If they did, teachers would feel more besieged than supported. Your job is to select several that are appropriate to your church and teachers at this time. Below is a list of all the suggestions in this chapter:

____________★"encouragement" to go to workshops
____________★monthly or quarterly teachers' meetings/workshops
____________★subscriptions to teachers' magazines
____________★teacher and student dedication service
____________phone calls to check in
____________teachers' bulletin board
____________publicize successes
____________teachers' communion service
____________basic resource library
____________helping hands
____________remembering teachers in public prayer
____________"hand on the back" encouragement
____________valentines
____________personal notes
____________a small gift
____________end of year teachers' party
____________appreciation flower
____________gift book at end of term

★The starred suggestions are the most effective ones. Every church needs to be providing at least two of the four for teachers. If you are not, select at least one to work on now, and plan to add a second later this year or early next year. Follow directions on "How to Get Started" in the part of the chapter that describes the support methods you select.

The unstarred suggestions might be called little things that mean so much. Each year you will need to use several of them. However, many of them will lose some of their effectiveness if done every year. So, for example, one year you may give teachers valentines. The next year you might give a small Christmas gift instead. The element of surprise makes your efforts look more spontaneous and genuine.

So check at least two of the starred (★) items and several of the unstarred items. Add to the list your own ideas about how to encourage, train, or inspire the teachers in your church. Make the necessary plans to provide all of these supports for your teachers this year.

Eight:

What You Can Expect, Ask for, and Forget About Getting from Your Minister

Small-church ministers, like the old country doctors, are expected to be able to do a variety of jobs. They need to preach inspiring (or at least not boring) sermons; baptize, marry, and bury members of the congregation; comfort the sick and shut-in; counsel people when their marriages are breaking up, their children are falling into "evil ways," or their lives are falling apart; organize the work and finances of the church; arbitrate church fights; and lead in the church's education ministry. Because each minister is an individual, each will excel in some areas and be less effective in others. That means that sometimes you may be blessed with a minister whose creativity and interest in education make the church school one of the most exciting parts of the life of the church, but whose financial leadership could take the church into bankruptcy. It also means that the next minister may draw in new members by her outstanding leadership in worship and inspirational preaching, while she is content to leave the church school to the lay folks.

Because ministers are individuals, it is impossible to write a single description of the role a minister should play in the church's education ministry. Instead, each congregation and its minister must describe together the role *that particular minister* will play in *that particular church*. Each role will be unique, but each will be made up of (1) some expectations of what any minister must do as part of being a minister, (2) the special gifts the particular minister offers, and (3) the special needs and gifts of the particular congregation.

As you define the role your minister will play, it is helpful to be clear about what is reasonable to expect from any minister, what kinds of roles a minister interested and trained in education might assume, and what is unreasonable to ask for or expect from any minister.

You Can Expect . . .

There are certain things you can expect from every minister. Regardless of their individual gifts and interests, when they accept the call to the ministry, ministers accept some responsibility for the education ministry of the church. Threfore, congregations have the right to expect any minister to:

(1) BE AN ENTHUSIASTIC SUPPORTER OF THE CHURCH SCHOOL. While a minister may not have equal zeal for, or even be in agreement with, every program or policy of the church school, there should be no doubt that he or she takes Christian education seriously. A minister with little interest in education, and no gifts as a teacher, can still be expected to give the support of an enthusiastic bystander. This support is evident in casual conversations around the church, the way announcements related to church school are made, and other little ways.

(2) KNOW WHAT IS HAPPENING IN THE CHURCH SCHOOL. Only the most interested ministers will keep up with what each class is studying unit by unit. But every minister needs to have basic knowledge of the church-school program. A minister needs to understand the overall purpose and educational approach of your church school, how students are divided for classes, who is teaching, and what curriculum is being used. This knowledge enables him or her to interpret the program to people when necessary, and to support it with some integrity.

(3) BE PRESENT AT CHURCH-SCHOOL ACTIVITIES WHEN POSSIBLE. The minister's presence proves his or her interest. If it is possible, a minister needs to be present during every church-school session, visiting different classes (of all ages), leading in classes occasionally, and talking with people working in education ministry. This may be all but impossible if a minister serves two or more chuches. In such cases the minister's attendance at programs and parties beyond the Sunday morning class can be essential.

(4) GIVE ADMINISTRATIVE SUPPORT TO CHRISTIAN EDUCATION. The minister, as the chief adminstrator of your church, serves on all the committees that set policy and coordinate programs. His or her support of education in this is essential. For example, the minister can, as a matter of routine, see that the choir does not begin holding regular rehearsals during church school, or that the budget committee does not cut the curriculum budget without finding out how the cut would affect the church school.

(5) EMPHASIZE THE IMPORTANCE OF EDUCATION IN SERMONS, ETC. In preaching, ministers are

constantly telling us what the Christian life is like. If their preaching indicates that growing in faith is an important part of being Christian, people will take education more seriously. Scripture is filled with calls to growth. These passages need to be read in worship and preached about frequently.

(6) *PRAY PUBLICLY AS WELL AS PRIVATELY FOR THE CHURCH'S EDUCATION MINISTRY*. When the youth are gone on a retreat, the congregation can pray together for their safety and Christian growth. At the beginning of the church-school year, pray together for its success. Offer thanksgiving for education work being done in your church. People pray about things they care about. As the prayer leader of the congregation, a minister can be expected to be praying about education in the church.

You Can Ask For . . .

In addition to the things you can expect of ALL ministers, there are a number of things you can ask your minister for. Ask for these things as ways of using special interests and talents. A few ministers would gladly try all of them. Some ministers will feel more competent to try one role than others. Other ministers have time for only a few of them. Some, in all honesty, have neither the interest, nor the ability, nor the time for any of them. If you ask your minister about one of these, you may get some suggestions of other ways she or he would like to be involved. Ask to explore possibilities, not to make demands. Some reasonable requests include asking your minister to:

(1) *BE A PART OF "THE RESPONSIBLE GROUP."* A minister with special interest in education can be a great asset to this group. From his or her reading, mail, and knowledge of Christian education, such a minister can point out useful resources, share new ideas, pass on denominational suggestions, and share in developing and implementing dreams. As minister, the person can interpret the work of "the responsible group" in education to others in the church.

(2) *HELP THE TEACHERS*. The help could come in different forms. Most ministers are glad to help teachers understand the content of their lessons or answer questions. If several classes study the same subject, you might ask the minister to lead an introductory lesson for the teachers on the subject they will teach during the coming quarter. Some ministers have the training and interest to serve as the "teacher of teachers" described in chapter 7. In this role, they could lead workshops and work with individual teachers in developing their teaching skills.

(3) *TEACH AN OCCASIONAL SHORT COURSE*. Many ministers enjoy teaching and teach well. Since they often do not want to be tied to one class or to teach every Sunday, short courses in different classes may be attractive to them and to the students. Thus, you may ask the minister to teach a four-week course on the formation of the Bible in the adult class, or a two-week unit on the sacraments in the children's class. The minister may teach alone or as part of a team.

You Can Forget . . .

There are a few things you simply cannot expect any minister to do. Some of these may look obvious, but what is obvious to one person needs explaining to another, because each community has its own myths about ministers. So, let me tell you that you can forget about:

(1) *USING THE MINISTER AS AN ON-CALL SUBSTITUTE FOR ALL CLASSES*. Ministers can no more teach a class without preparation than anyone else can. If a teacher calls in sick on Sunday morning, have another substitute ready with a pre-planned lesson, or combine classes. A minister's Sunday mornings tend to be hectic even with careful planning. There is no room for surprise teaching assignments.

(2) *EXPECTING THE MINISTER TO READ EACH CLASS'S LESSON EVERY SUNDAY*. There are not enough hours in the week for such activities. If a teacher calls for help on a specific lesson, it is reasonable to expect the minister to read that lesson and offer whatever help she or he can. It is *not* reasonable to expect the minister to read all lessons just in case advice, comments, and so forth, are needed.

(3) *EXPECTING MINISTERS TO BE CHURCH-SCHOOL EXPERTS*. Many people assume that graduates of seminaries have been taught the organization of church school and teaching skills as part of their training for the ministry. Unfortunately, this is not often true. Many seminaries neither require nor encourage such training. Some students, out of their own interest, do get such training and graduate as excellent teachers.

Other young ministers get the training after realizing their need for it while serving their first parishes. But you cannot expect that a minister will also be a knowledgeable church educator.

What to Do About It

Discuss it with your minister. Too often, laypeople have their own ideas of how the minister should be involved in the church school, and the minister has his or her ideas of how to relate to the church school. Each may have some good guesses about what the other is thinking. But no one ever actually talks about these ideas and hopes openly (unless a major crisis has resulted from differing, unvoiced expectations). There is little to be lost, and much to be gained, by openly discussing these role hopes and expectations in order to define a role that everyone is aware of and accepts.

Invite the minister and the "responsible group" to sit down together to discuss that minister's role in the church's education ministry. Give each person a copy of this chapter to read and think about before the meeting and to bring to the meeting as a reference. During the meeting, discuss each item listed under what you can expect, ask for, and forget about getting from a minister. Allow enough time for people to ask questions and agree or disagree with each item, but don't get bogged down on an item about which there is not total agreement. You will probably be able to move through the list of what you can expect from any minister fairly rapidly, but will want to spend more time on ways you might use the particular talents your minister offers. Ask your minister to outline her or his training in Christian education and to share how he or she wants to be involved in the church's education ministry. Discuss the possible roles outlined under what "you can ask for. . . ." Give lay people a chance to outline their ideas. As you discuss all these ideas and dreams and abilities, you will begin defining the role that your minister will play. The group may want to put this in writing. In some churches, however, a clear verbal agreement will be sufficient.

NOTE: If your church chooses its own ministers (instead of having one appointed by a bishop), and if the role the minister takes in education is important to your church, this discussion about roles should take place during the selection of each new minister. You may even want to campaign to get someone actively involved in Christian education on the committee to search for the new minister.

The Care and Feeding of Ministers

One last thing about a minister's involvement in education. Ministers, like teachers, grow and develop. Just as we need to take advantage of and honor talents they bring to us, we must work with them to increase their understanding and develop their underdeveloped talents. Any minister is capable of doing any of the jobs listed under "You can expect. . . ." If your minister is not active in such jobs, encourage him or her to get with it. Help them get started. If there is a book that describes the philosophy and purpose of the curriculum you are using, ask if they have a copy. If they do not, get them one. Enlist their support in specific ways, such as telling them that you are counting on them to help the budget committee understand the Christian education budget proposal. Ask them to preach a sermon related to Christian education. Invite them to participate in a class project. Let them know that it is important to you that they do these things. Thank them when they do begin fulfilling a role that is new to them.

If a minister knows little or nothing about education, encourage him or her to get some training. If there is a workshop you think your minister needs to attend, "encourage" her or his attendance just as you would that of any teacher. Invite the minister to join a group of teachers going to a workshop. (This has a double benefit. The minister gets some training and becomes part of the fellowship of the teachers, which the teachers appreciate.)

Finally, many ministers have a week or two a year to pursue "continuing education" to keep them growing as ministers. How they spend this time is usually their choice, but that choice can be influenced by suggestions. So let your minister know what areas you wish she or he would pursue.

If all this is done in a loving way by people who support them (rather than in a judgmental way by people who seem to be out to get them), most ministers will find such suggestions and invitations food for their growth, and will appreciate the good care you are giving them.

Nine:

Help from the Pros

Small churches have proved that a church can function quite well without the services of a regular minister. However, given the choice, almost any church prefers to have a minister. The same is true of professional Christian educators. Many, many churches work without them to offer fine education ministries. But educators do offer knowledge and skills that most churches would like to have available to them. In small churches, we usually assume that these services are out of reach since we cannot afford to hire a full-time Christian educator out of our limited budgets. This is not true. There are several other ways to get the services of professional Christian educators. Some of them have been mentioned in previous chapters. This chapter includes those ways, as well as others, to give a full picture of how small churches can "get help from the pros."

Use the Services Offered by Your Denomination's Area Staff

Most districts, presbyteries, conferences, associations, or regional staffs include a professional Christian educator whose job is to help churches under that jurisdiction provide the best education ministry possible. Often they carry out this task by setting up workshops and cooperative ministries (for example, area youth retreats) to which members of individual churches are invited. By all means, take advantage of as many of these services as possible. But staff educators are generally also available on request to help individual churches with the education ministry of their particular church. While they cannot provide full educator services to each church in their area, these people can help you in several specific ways.

(1) *A staff educator can help you solve a particular problem.* If, for example, your church has decided to remodel the old fellowship hall and wants to make it usable for church school as well as church suppers, you might ask the staff educator to meet with the planning committee to help design the space to fit your particular education needs. Or, if you have come to an absolute standstill in youth ministry with no idea which way to go to get things moving again, call on the staff educator. He or she may come meet with you to evaluate the situation and figure out some new directions. Staff educators can also be very helpful when you are considering curriculum changes. They can show you what is available and help you select materials appropriate to your church. This kind of problem-solving help can mean the difference between getting hopelessly bogged down and rising to meet new challenges.

(2) *A staff educator can suggest resources.* Because they try to keep up with the Christian education materials coming out, staff educators can often point out resources that will meet specific needs. Therefore if your church has decided to do sex education with the youth, you could ask the staff educator to suggest two or three sets of materials from which you can make a selection. Ask about resources related to a specific topic, or a particular age group, or a special situation. In some denominations you can borrow many resources from the area offices. In others, the staff educator may give you a list of resources and suggest places where you will find the items on that list.

(3) *A staff educator can lead an occasional teacher-training event in your church for your teachers.* There are obviously limits to how much of this kind of work a person with wide responsibilities for a large number of churches can do in each church. But if you have a specific need that you think your staff person could meet particularly well, ask. If, for example, you are joining several tiny children's classes to form a broadly graded class, you might ask the staff educator to lead a training session on teaching that class. If you are starting a new curriculum, the staff educator might lead a session introducing the curriculum and showing teachers how to use it most effectively. Both of these are special situations in which a staff educator can provide very useful one-time training leadership.

(4) *A staff educator can put you in touch with people who can help.* In smaller denominational regions, the staff educator will know who among the people he or she serves has which skills and talents. In larger regions, such information can be found recorded in files or even on computers in the office. In either case, the staff educator can often put you in touch with people with the specific talents you need. In the case of the church starting a broadly graded children's class, a staff educator, instead of coming personally, could name a person

who has been teaching such a group very successfully for several years. You could then ask that person to come train your teachers.

A CHALLENGE: In small churches, particularly rural ones, we often hesitate to use the help these outsiders offer, especially if they are labeled "consultants." We wonder how much they will really understand US and OUR SITUATION. Such hesitation only hurts us, because it limits the kind of services and input we are willing to receive as we build our education ministries. "Consultants" bring only information and suggestions. How much use we make of those is up to us. The church, not the "consultant," is in control. So do not automatically set aside suggestions to get in touch with a person who has a specific skill you need.

Get Help from a Christian Educator in a Neighboring Church

Many Christian educators serving single churches are willing to offer limited advice and services to smaller churches in the area. One way to get their help is to contract for particular services, such as leading quarterly teacher-training workshops at your church (see chapter 8). Contracts have the advantage of putting in print what is expected and offered by both the church and the educator. Threfore, they reduce the chance that either the educator will be or feel abused, or that the church will fear it is abusing the educator.

It is also possible to develop a non-contract friendship with an educator. Such a friendship might include phone conversations to get information on specific resources or possible solutions to particular problems. You might also ask your educator-friend to lead an occasional workshop in your church (provide a small honorarium for workshops). The key to the success of such a friendship is openness about what is being asked for and the freedom for the educator to draw lines when necessary.

For instance, while serving a large United Church of Christ congregation, I enjoyed such a friendship with a smaller Lutheran church in the same city. It began with my friendship with Ruth, a dedicated Lutheran layperson with whom I worked on a number of city-wide Christian education projects. Though I knew very little about Lutheran education in particular, I was able to answer questions about where to find useful resources beyond denominational curricula, suggest some solutions to education problems they were struggling with, and explain an unfamiliar teaching activity or two. All of this was done in occasional (never more than monthly), brief phone conversations with Ruth. I led one teacher-training session for them on how to plan a lesson, for which they gave me a small honorarium. Because I knew that my help was valued and that I could say no whenever I needed to, I enjoyed doing what I could for this church. One of my treasures is a small ceramic Madonna and Child Ruth gave me when I moved.

Find Help at Nearby Seminaries and Colleges That Teach Christian Education Courses

Most seminaries have at least one professor of Christian education. Many have more. In addition, many church colleges and universities offer courses in Christian education and, therefore, employ trained educators. Both professors and students in such schools can provide educator services.

Professors can become educator-friends much like the educator in a neighboring church can. Some professors are employed part-time by their schools and look for part-time work in nearby churches as an economic necessity. Others who do not need the money want such a relationship in order to keep in touch with the local church and to avoid becoming "ivory tower academics." Professors may contract to teach a specific course in their area of expertise or to lead teacher workshops.

Students training themselves to be Christian educators are often anxious for opportunities to get experience. They can be outstanding youth fellowship advisors or church-school teachers. Some students will take on such work as part of their school's volunteer program, or as a project or field-work for which they receive academic credit. Other students may need a small fee to help them cover their school expenses. In either case, both the church and the students are winners when students go to work in a church's education ministry.

Hire a Christian Educator Part-Time

So far we have been identifying ways to get occasional help from professionals. Occasional help is very useful and can save the day in crisis situations, but it will never get the results that the ongoing work of a professional can bring your church. An educator who is in your church regularly can help solve lots of little problems before they become unmanageable. Educators can offer suggestions that add richness to individual classes and to the whole education ministry. They can contribute to dreaming about opportunities you would like to offer and help make those dreams a reality over the years. While an educator does not reduce the work required of lay people, and may even increase it, he or she can make that work more effective and satisfying. And while educators cannot perform miracles, like instantly resuscitating dead church schools, they generally do improve the church schools they serve. So there are many advantages to engaging the services of an educator on a regular basis.

This is not impossible for small churches, because there are many professional Christian educators who, for a variety of reasons, do not want full-time work. A mother with young children may want to work part-time to keep involved in her profession while protecting time to care for her children. As mentioned earlier, a professor of Christian education may want to work part-time in a congregation. A graduate student often needs to work part-time while studying for advanced degrees in Christian education. As I write this book, I am working part-time (two days per week) in a rural church of two hundred members. The situation keeps me active in the church but allows time for serious writing in the field of Christian education. And there are others with still other reasons for seeking part-time work.

Therefore, it is not an improbable dream that your small church could find and hire a part-time Christian educator. To explore this possibility, invite the denomination's staff educator in your area to help you draw up a job description, proposed salary, and so forth. Many denominations have guidelines to help you in this. The staff educator can also tell you about educator placement services that could help you find the right person. Area ministers, the staff educator, and other educators you know can also suggest names of people you might want to contact about the job.

WARNINGS: There is a saying among church professionals that there is no part-time church work, only work you are part-paid for. Most laugh when they say it, but they are serious about the problem. The church that offers part-time pay, but demands full-time work, is setting up itself and the educator it hires for trouble. So be honest with yourselves and with prospective educators about what you expect for the salary you are offering. Check regularly with any educator you employ to be sure the job has not outgrown the original agreement.

A second warning is to overcome the temptation to hire an educator who has no training or certification for the job. Such people may be charming, dedicated to the church, and willing to work cheaply. However, they have not learned skills related to teacher training, studied the ways people grow in their faith, or explored and evaluated the mass of resources and curricula available today. You get what you pay for. You will generally profit more from a little time with a professional educator than you will from lots of time with an untrained educator.

Hire a Christian Educator in Cooperation with Other Churches

One other way to get regular professional help is to join forces and finances with one or more other churches. Together you can hire a full-time educator to serve each church according to prearranged agreements. It is easiest for churches of the same denomination to share an educator. However, churches of different denominations who have a history of working together locally often share an educator quite successfully. Such ecumenical arrangements are most common in very small towns or rural areas.

It is possible to share only in funding the educator. In that situation, each contributing church gets the agreed-upon percentage of the educator's time to use as that church and the educator see fit. A plan for the educator's use of Sunday time will need to be agreed on from the start. An annual evaluation of the work done, the job description, and the salary is the only further contact required between the churches.

However, many churches who share an educator find that there are other ways they can share for their mutual benefit. For example, seven small churches under the leadership of their educator sponsor one big Vacation Bible Day Camp instead of seven small vacation Bible schools. During this camp they combine all their best resources to create a more exciting and educational experience than any one church could offer alone. Over nearly ten years of working together, the same churches have profited by cooperating on officer training, sponsoring a Junior High fellowship, providing special opportunities for Senior High youth, sharing a communicant's class, passing around curriculum materials to save money, and sponsoring some joint teacher workshops. All of this indicates that you may want to encourage a shared educator to develop ways of cooperating in your education ministries. (Two ways to do this are to set aside some of his or her time for such activities, and to develop plans for funding such activities.)

In summary, you are not without help. There are many ways for a small church to get the services of professional Christian educators. To get these services you must decide what you want, and then you must go out and find it. The assignment below is included to enable you to accomplish these two important tasks.

Assignment

(1) To evaluate your needs for professional help, look at the list below of some helps professionals can offer. First, simply check those kinds of help you think you do need. Then, rank the items you checked, marking the one you need most as "1," the next as "2," and so forth.

______help individual teachers do better jobs
______teacher training for teachers as a group
______help in planning overall education ministry
______leadership in youth ministry
______selecting and getting curriculum and other resources
______help with administrative work like class divisions and use of space
______problem solving (when needed)
______(others)

(2) Keeping in mind the needs you identified, send out individuals or teams to find out what help you can get.

(A) Call or visit the person charged with education ministry in your district, association, or presbytery. Tell them about the needs you identified, and ask what help you might get from them and others in your denomination. Ask them specifically whether you can get from them the help outlined in this chapter. Also ask them about other sources of help you might investigate.

(B) Make a list of all the local seminaries and colleges that might teach Christian education courses. In some areas, this list may be very short. But in many areas, the list will be interestingly long. Call each school and talk to the person who teaches Christian education. (It will take some work to find the name of this person and then to reach them. Persistence is the key.) Tell them about the needs you identified and ask what help you might find at the school. Ask about the specific sources of help mentioned in this chapter. Keep notes on their suggestions.

(C) Make a list of professional educators working in your area. There is no one place to get this information. If you think a church might employ an educator, call and ask them if they do. Then get the educator's name. Ask your minister if he or she knows of any educators. If you personally know one of these people, tell them about your needs and ask if they can help in any way, or know an educator who might.

(3) Hear reports on the research done in step two above. Discuss the possibilities identified, as well as the possibilities of hiring a part-time educator or sharing an educator. Make plans to use the professional help you have located.

Ten:

Getting Maximum Use of Minimum Space and Equipment

Let me begin with a few words to clarify what this chapter is, and what it is not. It is not an exhaustive text on planning the use of space and selecting proper furnishings and equipment for that space. There are no statistics about the number of square feet of floor space needed by students of different ages, no charts showing the proper heights for tables and chairs for students of each age, no suggestions about long-lasting wall coverings and the results of using different colors in rooms of different sizes, and no suggestions about the kinds of furnishings and equipment that are appropriate to different kinds of classes. All of that is very useful information, but is beyond the scope of this chapter. Indeed, it would be a book in itself. (Your denomination or the curriculum you use may offer such a book that is written with your particular approach to education in mind. If such a book is available, get a copy. It will be useful over and over as you care for and furnish your education space.)

This chapter is a look at some of the space and equipment problems peculiar to small churches. It offers some solutions that have proved useful in other small churches, and some suggestions about how to tackle the task of providing usable space and the equipment needed to provide education ministry in small churches.

Using Your Space Effectively

Printed church-school curricula generally assume that we are operating our classes in a building similar to a school building. This is seldom true for us in small churches. However, that does not mean that we have no space to work in. Most small churches have enough space to meet their education needs. We must recognize, however, what space IS available and how we can most effectively use every square foot of it. Almost every church has certain kinds of space. Each space offers a specific set of opportunities and problems.

The Sanctuary

If a church has only one small building, it will almost surely be a sanctuary and therefore be designed and furnished for public worship. Worship and education are different activities and generally require different kinds of space. However, they can, and often must, get along in the same room.

The main problem in using sanctuaries for education is that pews are bolted to the floor. This severely limits what can be done with most of the floor area in the building. The easiest use of these pews is as seating for a class that prefers a lecture/lesson every Sunday. That is exactly what many small churches use their sanctuaries for during church school. But there are some problems even with this. Few classes will fill a sanctuary, but many students will sit scattered throughout the room anyway. This hardly creates a feeling of closeness and unity. In fact, it often makes it difficult for the teacher to be heard.

The solution is simple. Ask people to sit together in one section of the room. To encourage this choose a particular space within the sanctuary that fits the class. The choir pews may be the perfect place for a smaller lecture class. A larger class may be better seated on the first pews of the sanctuary, with the teacher speaking from a small movable lectern that puts her or him closer to the class than most pulpits do. Another class might prefer to gather in pews on one side of the sanctuary near the rear. The teacher of this class would stand between the pews just in front of the students. Ask the class to decide which section they prefer. You may even need to move around some. For example, the back corner near opened windows may be breezily comfortable in the summer, but drafty in the winter.

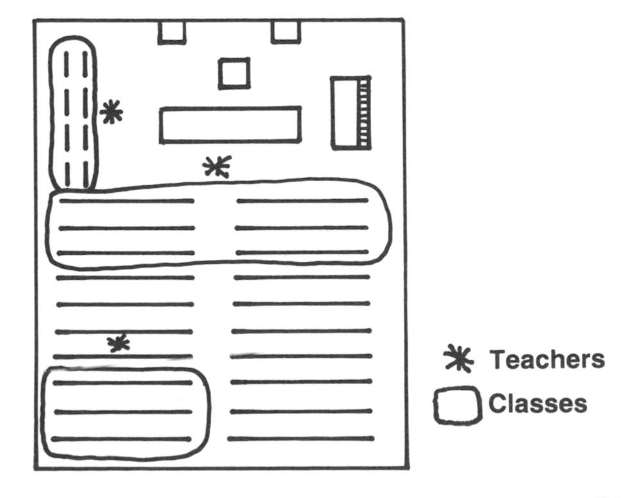

If you are dealing with ritualists, be aware of what you are asking. It may be more important to them to sit in a particular place than to hear the lesson. Therefore, you may need to gather the class near their "regular seats." If you insist that they move, prepare for resistance. (But do not necessarily prepare to give in. Ritualists can develop new rituals.)

The rows of permanent pews present a bigger challenge if you need space for a class that wants to discuss and research and learn actively. Even discussion is all but impossible if people are seated in rows. Classes of such learners will need space beyond the pews. An adult class may be able to form a square or circle of chairs using the front pew as part of the circle. Folding tables could be set up if the class needs table work space to do written work. The chairs and tables used need to be stored in a nearby hall or room for convenience. Though it requires a little extra work, arranging seating in this way can make the difference between the success and failure of a discussion class.

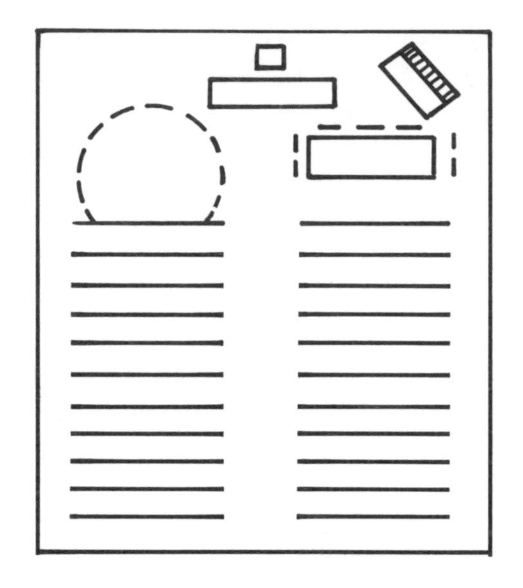

This was clearly demonstrated by one class of adults who decided to become more of a discussing group than the listening group they had been. As they sat in a circle in the front corner of the sanctuary, they enjoyed sharing ideas and had some good debates. But they also got lazy about setting up chairs and were soon sitting in rows on the pews again. Then there were complaints that they had fallen back into their listening ways. As they talked about their problem they realized that it was impossible for their group to discuss while sitting in rows in the sanctuary. For too many years they had been taught to sit and listen there. Once they set up the circle of chairs, they were again free to discuss and take active part in their class.

No matter where you place a class in the sanctuary, the fact that you are in the sanctuary presents some potential problems. Shortly after church school ends, the same room will be used for worship. That means the organist may want to practice a few minutes, someone will arrive with flowers to arrange, the minister may bring sermon notes to the pulpit, and early worshipers might interrupt your class. Much of this can be avoided if clear expectations are set down. The responsible group needs to appeal to the organist, minister, and congregation to avoid these interruptions. Ask for this as their support of the church's education ministry. Enlist the minister's help in reminding people of this when necessary. Often the hardest situation to deal with is that of the early worshipers, especially on a rainy or cold day. One church solves this problem with a homemade wooden sign placed at the rear entry door. The sign, announcing "Church School in session," is placed in the aisle near the doorway until class ends, when it is moved. Early worshipers are free to enter and quietly take a seat while the sign is out. Once the sign is put away, conversation is allowed in the sanctuary.

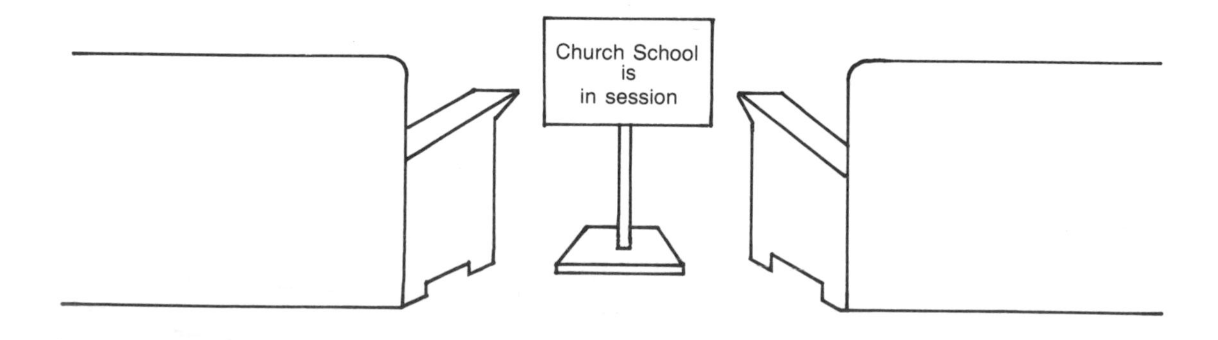

Another solution to these problems is to use wing rooms rather than the sanctuary. Many small churches with older buildings have such wing rooms near the front of their sanctuaries. These small rooms can often be closed off with curtains, folding doors, or room dividers. When opened, they are used for seating large crowds of worshipers at weddings, funerals, homecoming, and other important worship events. But they can also provide excellent classroom space.

Tables and chairs can be arranged as in any classroom. Bookshelves, bulletin boards, chalk boards, and similar displays can be set up on the walls that are not seen from the sanctuary. When the space is needed for worship, the tables are folded away, and the chairs are arranged in rows like pews. Displays on the walls not seen from sanctuary pews can be left in place (1).

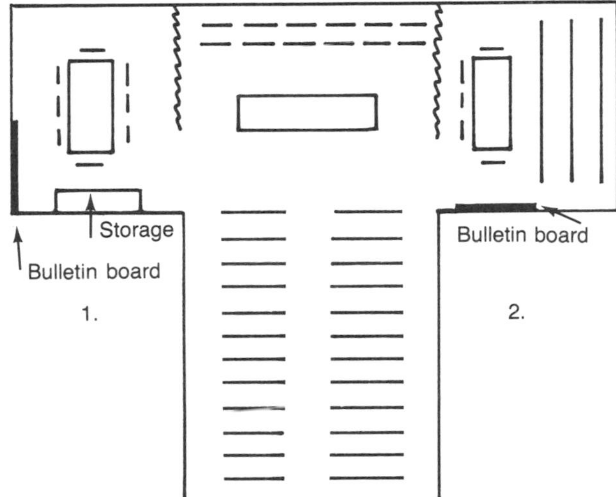

If your wing rooms are filled with bolted-down pews, ask the proper group about the possibility of removing them to create more usable rooms. If this is not allowed, the space can be used by a lecture class or, if there is space in front of the first pew, a circle of chairs and even a table can be set up for a small class. Again, wall space unseen in the sanctuary can be used for storage and displays (2).

The Hall

The second most common church space is a large room with an adjoining kitchen. Often called "the fellowship hall" or simply "the hall," this room is used for many things. It is the party room for wedding receptions, family night suppers, showers, and seasonal church parties. Scouts, 4-H, an exercise class, the garden club, community civic action committees, and the bloodmobile may use it during the week. The youth fellowship, with or without official blessing, may play basketball or foursquare in it on Sunday evening. And it may be the most available room for church-school teaching. To use such a hall wisely and efficiently takes some careful planning.

Any room can be used more easily by one group at a time than by two or more groups at the same time. Two groups distract each other by sound and sight. While it is fairly easy to separate groups visually, it is both difficult and expensive to keep their noises from distracting each other. Therefore, consider putting one large class in the hall, rather than two or three small ones. This is yet another reason to try broadly graded children's classes. Instead of chopping the hall up into several tiny classrooms just big enough for a table and chairs, and so close to others that we must always be quiet, we can spread activities across the entire room. Chairs are set around the piano for singing loud, happy songs of praise. There is adequate room to put on a play with cardboard box scenery painted during class. Tables for divided activities can be far enough apart to separate the groups (because students know what is going on in other groups in the open room, they will not be as distracted as they would be by unknown activities on the other side of a curtain).

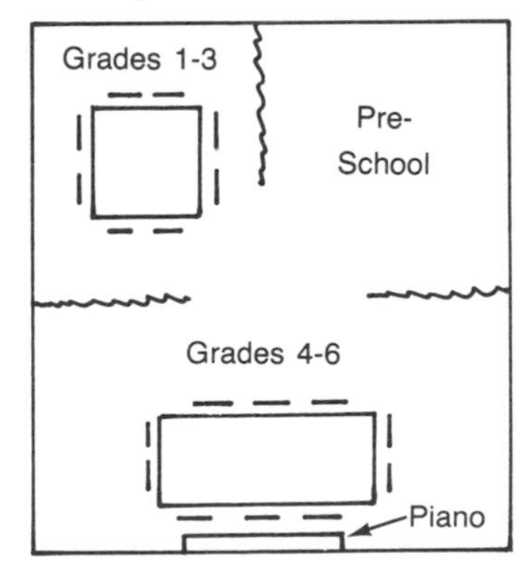

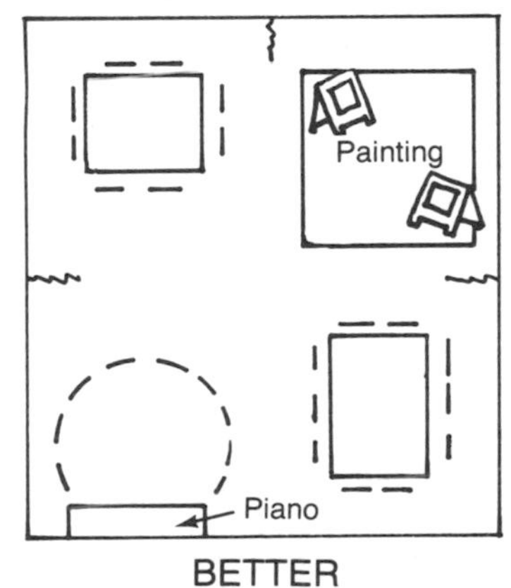

BETTER

Combine small classes into one large class to use "the hall" most comfortably

If you must divide the hall up for use by separate classes, put similar classes in the room. Instead of putting the preschoolers and an adult class in a divided room, put the preschool and the children, or two adult classes, together. The noise in each of the two children's classes will block out the noise of the other. The two adult classes will be quiet enough that folding doors will give them the sound protection they need. There are, however, no folding doors that will keep the adults from hearing the noise of a nursery-kindergarten in the other end of the room.

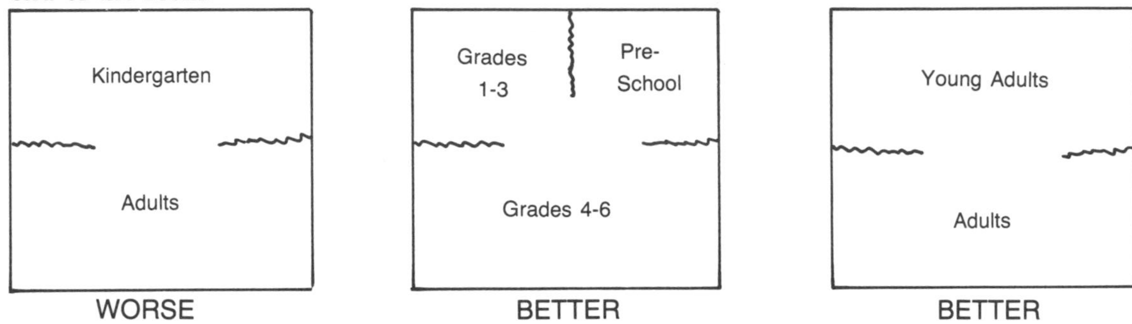

If you must divide the room, put similar classes in each section

Whether you use the hall as one room or subdivide it, the use it gets at different times of the week requires some careful planning. The friction that develops when the Scouts borrow the last of the youth class's glue, or when the ladies' auxiliary tea must begin by picking up scattered nursery toys, is avoidable. Two things are especially helpful: (1) storage, and (2) rearrangement plans.

Every group that uses the room regularly needs its own storage space and the assurance that it will not be plundered, no matter how just the cause. The kind of storage space needed will depend on the group. An adult class may be able to keep study books, some extra Bibles and songbooks, and a box of pencils on a small bookshelf. The Scout troop may need a trunk to store knotting ropes, their flags, some balls, craft supplies, and so forth. A preschool class may need storage space for toys.

There are as many different ways of providing such storage as there are groups. Here are a few I have encountered:

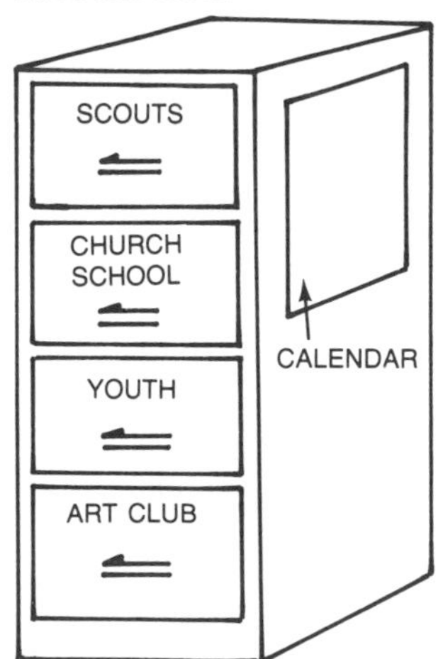

Invest in a secondhand file cabinet (businesses often sell their old ones while they are still in very acceptable condition, at a price considerably less than that of a new one). Assign each group a drawer with a clear label. These wide, deep drawers can hold a nearly endless variety of things, from files, to books, to art supplies, to small recreation equipment, to diapering needs. The space can further aid cooperation if a calendar is posted on the side for all groups to record their plans for using the hall.

Scout troops and nursery classes often have bulky equipment and toys that will not fit in drawers or on shelves. One way to provide space for such equipment is to build in long boxes along the wall. Each box is topped by a cushioned lid so it can serve as a seat as well as a storage box. This may be a cooperative project for the Scouts (making the boxes) and the women's groups (making cushions for the lids).

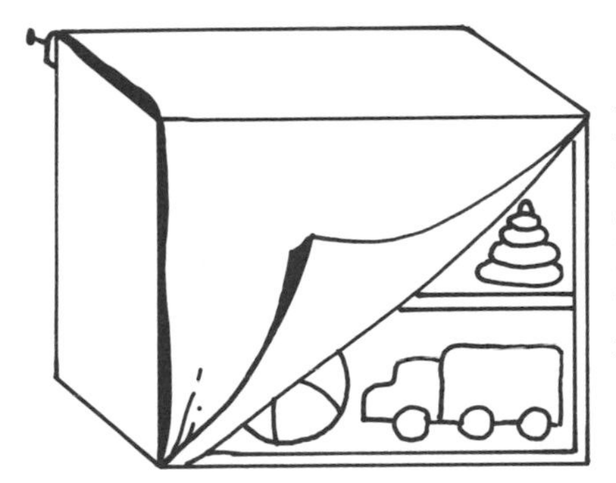

Another solution is to build some deep bookshelves big enough to hold the toys and equipment in question. To get the contents out of sight when they are not in use, tack a piece of heavy fabric to the back of the top shelf. Let the fabric fall in front of the shelf when not in use. Flip it back to make contents easily available when wanted. A group wanting an exceptionally attractive room could turn the fabric over into a banner with Christian symbols or messages.

One church designed a large cabinet that especially met their needs. A carpenter-member built it for them for the cost of the materials. The lower right section included space for a roll of butcher paper, which was set on a dime store Lazy Susan so that the paper could be easily rolled off. Beside it, a series of small shelves held colored paper, pencils, brushes, and supplies all classes shared. The other sections were fitted with movable shelves. In the lower left section the church's record player, filmstrip projector, and other A-V equipment were stored. The top sections were assigned, one to each of the two classes that met in the room, for their own books and supplies. This space was diverse enough to hold almost any project either class was working on.

If everyone who uses the room has a place to store things, the room will be neater for all. But there is still potential trouble in major room arrangement. If teachers arrive expecting to find their room set up pretty much as they left it, but find the room filled with rows of chairs left from a community meeting during the week, their whole morning will be chaotic. The simplest solution to this is to decide on a standard room arrangement and ask all groups to leave the room in that pattern. If the church school classes are the most regular users of the room, your standard arrangement may be church school class arrangement. However, if other groups use the room weekly, there may be some "middle-ground arrangement" that is fair to all.

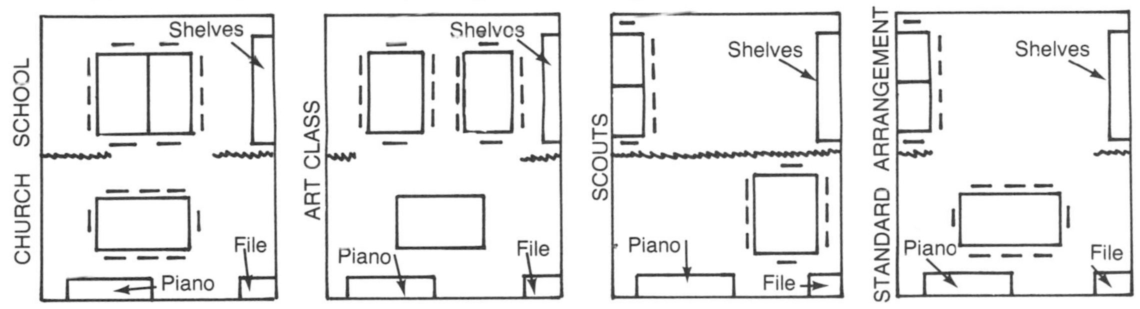

A yearly meeting of representatives of all groups that use the room regularly can avoid much of the friction. At this meeting, assign storage space to each group, make agreement about which supplies and equipment can be shared and which cannot, and set a pattern for how the room is to be left by each user. Being clear about this makes sharing the space more pleasant for everyone.

Lots of Little Rooms

Churches with older buildings often are stuck with a wing full of tiny rooms. These rooms were built in the days when classes of all ages sat in rows of chairs or never moved from their seats around one table. If you dream of more active classes, this setup may look rather grim. It can be, but . . .

If the money and interest are available, tear down some of those walls to create larger, more versatile spaces.

If such radical remodeling is not possible, consider assigning several rooms to one active class. Create a suite of rooms—a "together room" with piano and a circle of chairs to use for singing, group worship, and discussions; a library room with reference books and tables for group study; a project room for painting murals or planning plays; and so forth. Each Sunday the class can move around between the rooms. "Large" classes can divide to work in different rooms at the same time.

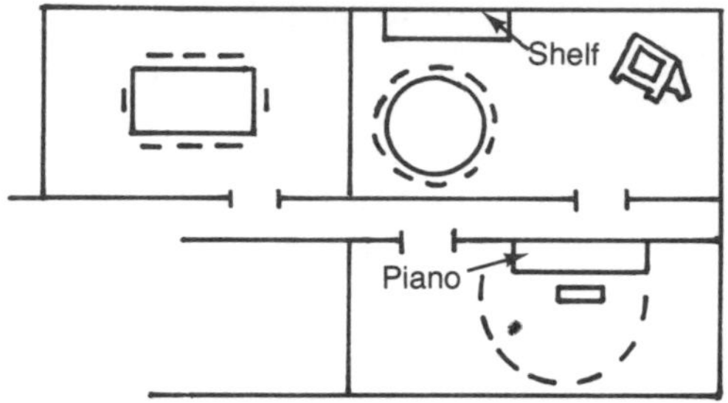

Finally, a small room can be just right for a small class. For example one of the most inviting church-school rooms I have seen is the size of a storage closet. That it happens to have a stained-glass window in one wall helps. The teacher, who meets with a maximum of two kindergarten children, painted the room soft yellow, put down a patch of light green shag carpet, removed everything but three small chairs, a tiny child's table and a bookshelf, and hung a big picture of Jesus and the children on the wall. The result is a very pleasant corner of the church that the children claim as their special place. In it there is just enough room for three people to read stories, work puzzles, draw pictures, sing, and play games.

You Can Have Too Much Space

Yes, even in small churches you can have too much space. In a fit of optimism, members may have built a building with room for growth that has never come. Or the drop in the birthrate may have left your once-crowded rooms somewhat empty. Whatever the circumstances, it is just as crucial to use too much space wisely as it is to use too little space efficiently.

A small class using a large room faces several problems. For one thing, they face the discouragement of feeling that they really should fill the room. If they spread out trying to fill the void, the emptiness is not only emphasized, but it keeps them from enjoying the closeness a small group offers. If students are children, too much space can make discipline difficult. All that space begs to be run and yelled in.

If a small class must use a large room, create a smaller space within the space. Use available room dividers, even if no one is meeting on the other side. Use furniture to create boundaries. For example, a bookshelf (even a low one students can see over) can be turned across a room, or in an adult class, the chairs can be gathered in one corner of the room around a table or near a worship center.

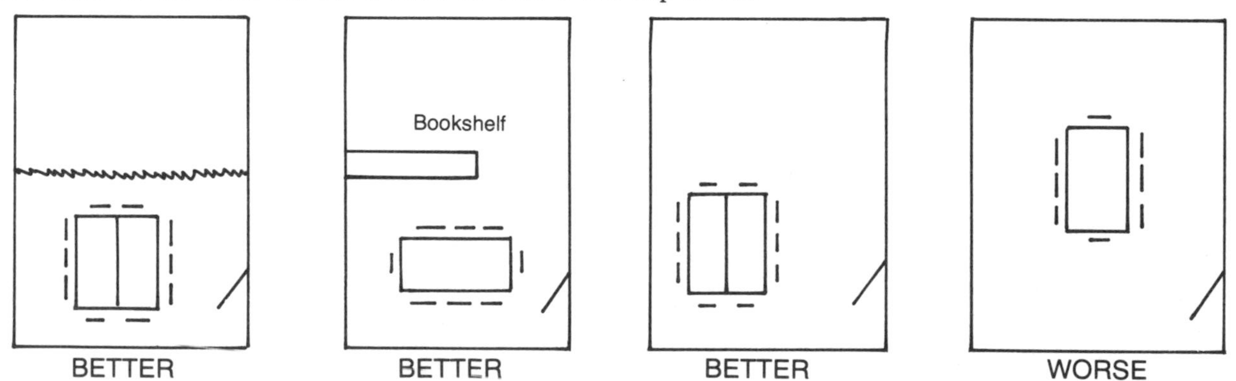

If you have too many rooms, do not use them. Simply close off a hall or wing for a while (in this age of energy conservation this has some obvious fringe benefits). Use rooms in one area so that people are aware of the bustle and activity in that area rather than feeling they are rattling around in the whole church.

General Truisms About Space

★ Adults will see to it that unattractive space is fixed, if they must use that space. Therefore, if the ceiling is falling or the heat is undependable, assign that room to an adult class. They will see that the space is made more livable.

★ Avoid, *if possible,* letting classes lay permanent claim to specific spaces. That way, classes can be placed according to their current needs instead of "where they have always met." Consequently, if the youth class needs the biggest room in the building one year, but a much smaller one the following year, their needs can be met.

★ Match the space to the age. Some spaces that are totally unacceptable to one age can be perfectly delightful to another—especially if you take advantage of the area's features. For example, basement rooms with exposed furnace ducts and peeling plaster walls would require total remodeling for use by an adult class or nursery. But if they are named "the catacombs," some Christian symbol graffiti painted here and there on the walls, and introduced to the students with a study of the early church in the catacombs, the youth might take great pleasure in developing this area and studying in it.

★ Little things like fresh paint and a "cared-for look," say a lot. Remember the storage closet kindergarten room that was so inviting? In another church of the same size, there was a larger room stocked with all sorts of beautiful wooden toys left from "bigger" days. But grayish walls, old pictures hung at adult instead of child eye-level, and a sense of dustiness made that room much less appealing than the happy little closet. So concentrate on making the most of what is available. What you have can be exactly what you need.

★ When you do redecorate any part of your building that might be used in education, consult a professional church educator! A church educator can help you identify potential education uses of a given space and suggest things to consider in doing your remodeling. For example, if you are planning to carpet "the hall" to help acoustics, the educator might point out that this would eliminate the use of the room for indoor recreation by children and youth and suggest that you explore some other ways of improving the acoustics.

Assignment

(1) Draw a floor plan of your building. It need not be to exact measurements, but do get it roughly to scale. Include EVERYTHING. Overlook no closets, nooks, storage areas, etc.

(2) In each space on your floor plan, mark its use(s). Then, answer the following questions together:

—Is any space unused or underused? Look particularly at storage areas. Have any potentially useful rooms gathered junk until they have become "storage closets"?

—Is any space overused? For example, is "the hall" being used as both parlor and gym? If so, can some groups be put into another space to the satisfaction of all?

—Are there groups that could be more comfortable in another space? Make some changes if necessary.

—Are there ways you could make space more usable—such as added storage or sprucing up?

What You Put in the Space

In furnishing a church school, we are always in a tension between wanting to provide the best possible equipment for the present, and fearing that our purchases will not be of much long-range use and therefore can be skimped on. It is both a frustrating and a healthy tension to work within. Working within that tension, I believe you need to:

(1) Buy only what you cannot make. Teaching equipment, from bulletin boards, to easels, to screens, to felt boards, and even write-on maps, can be made at home. Full directions for these and other kinds of equipment are contained in *Better Media for Less Money* by Donn McGuirk (order from National Teacher Education Project, 6947 East MacDonald Drive, Scottsdale, Arizona 85253. Cost: $7.25). If you find this book useful, you may want to invest $10.00 in *Better Media Volume Two,* which describes forty-three different money saving projects. Making equipment for the church school is one way to involve those who are not teachers in education ministry. Enlist their help, and publicly recognize such contributions in ways that indicate the work is important and appreciated.

(2) *Buy minimum needs.* Do not buy for projected growth. Instead, buy as growth comes.

(3) *Buy multi-purpose adjustable equipment.* If a table, for instance, has folding legs that can be adjusted to different heights, it can be used in the adult room this year, a children's class next year, and folded away for compact storage when it is not needed at all. Such a table costs more than one without folding, adjustable legs, but it will save money in the long run, because you will not be buying special tables for each new situation.

(4) *Spend the money to buy high-quality furniture and equipment.* Well-made tables and chairs are expensive, but they are made to stand up for years of hard use—and church furniture does get hard use. It is tempting to buy cheaper items, but doing this seldom pays off. The temptation is particularly strong when buying record players and other audio-visual equipment. Cheaper machines sold in discount stores or designed "for operation by children" generally do not last long and cannot be repaired. Institutional machines cost much more but last longer and can be repaired and serviced when needed. Most institutional-quality machines can be easily operated by our machine-wise children today. So buy quality equipment. You save money in the long run.

But do shop around to get the best price. Once you have decided exactly what you want, check prices at several different places. You may be surprised at the differences. A school supply house may give you the same big discount they give public schools and so beat out projector prices at your local camera store. A large discount catalog may offer identical brand-name equipment cheaper yet. Some denominations sell church-school furnishings and equipment at reduced prices no profit-making retailer can offer. Therefore, the time spent shopping around can save significant sums of money.

Once equipment is purchased and in use, it needs to be reevaluated at least annually. If a class of ten students has twenty chairs, move those extra chairs out. Put them somewhere where they are needed or put them in storage until they are needed again.

Audio-Visual Equipment

Providing audio-visual equipment can seem especially difficult to small churches. Curricula call for at least record players, cassette recorders, and filmstrip projectors, and sometimes more. But few of these get weekly use. Lots of equipment gathers more dust than use. And it is expensive!

Below is a list of what experience has taught me are the pieces of audio-visual equipment useful in a church of any size.

ESSENTIAL ITEMS (LISTED IN ORDER OF PRIORITY)

(1) filmstrip projector (do not pay extra for a slide adapter because they seldom work satisfactorily)
(2) record player
(3) cassette recorder
(4) slide projector
(5) 16 mm movie projector

NICE BUT NOT NECESSARY

- home movie camera
- home movie projector
- video-tape recorder
- video-tape camera
- overhead projector

That is a long, expensive list, but every church, with a little exploration, can gain access to almost every item on this list, because most of them need not be purchased. They can be borrowed from a variety of sources.

—Church members. Many families own equipment, from cassette recorders, to movie cameras, to video-tape systems, which they would be willing to loan to the church. Some may even have equipment to donate.

—Public schools. Some schools have policies encouraging the use of their equipment by community groups. Teachers and school officials in your church can most easily find out what is available in your schools.
—Private schools (day schools, colleges, graduate, and specialty schools).
—Church resource centers.
—Your denomination's area office.
—Businesses. Some companies have projectors with which they train employees and sell products. They may consider it good community relations to loan these out occasionally. Church members can consult companies they work in about this possibility.
—Public libraries.
—Technical schools or community colleges.
—Other churches. Some neighboring churches even make agreements to buy different equipment and share what they have. One might buy an overhead projector, while the other buys a 16 mm projector. Each is free to borrow from the other.

Assignment

(1) Make a list of audio-visual equipment that is available and in working order in your church. If you find any that is unusable and unrepairable, throw it away! There is no reason to keep it cluttering up your space.
(2) Compare your list of equipment with the list in this chapter.
(3) Assign members of your group to research each of the possible sources listed on the previous page to find sources of the equipment you lack. Learn what procedures and rules must be followed to borrow equipment from each source.
(4) Compile the results of your research into a list of equipment and the way it is available to your church. If you have been unable to locate a source for any of the essential equipment, make plans to buy it.

SAMPLE LIST

Filmstrip Projector—in office closet.
Record Player—Church owns two. One in office closet; one in children's classroom.
Cassette Recorder—borrow from Jones's, McRoy's, or Elton's.
Slide Projector—Jim Kane will lend his Carousel.
16 mm Movie Projector—borrow from public library. Make request two weeks in advance.
Home movie camera & projector—Kim Jones volunteers to help classes make movies using her equipment.
Video-tape camera & recorder—borrow from public school. Gene Ames is familiar with the equipment at Stanback School. He will borrow it and operate it when needed. Give him several weeks' notice.
Overhead Projector—Presbytery's office.

You will be surprised to see how much sophisticated teaching equipment is available for use in your education ministry.

(5) Give a copy of this list to each teacher and save several copies for future reference.

Eleven:

Those @#*#@ Opening Assemblies

Churches fight, struggle, and feud over many different things. Some churches are forever battling over the music they use or do not use. Others bicker about the use of the building—especially the kitchen. Still others are constantly divided over church-school curriculum. My experience is that most of the churches that have opening assemblies are fated to ongoing struggles related to them.

Of the seven small churches I recently served in Orange County, only one had an assembly that was enjoyed by all. Two had no assembly, and the remaining four were always fussing about and tinkering with theirs. In each church, some people would not think of starting church school without an assembly. To them, the assembly was every bit as important and meaningful as the classroom lessons. They tended to consider those who dissented nearly heretics. The dissenters, on the other hand, complained that this "mini-worship service led by amateurs" was a boring waste of time. They preferred to devote all of the church-school time to studying, and save worship for the morning preaching service. They complained that the same announcements were made in opening assembly and at the worship service. In general, they considered supporters of the assembly a bunch of fuddy-duddies who were holding on to an outdated ritual.

In short, it seems that the beginning point of dealing constructively with opening assemblies is to agree to disagree about them. If we can accept the fact that faithful Christians have, and are probably going to continue to have, radically different ideas about the value of opening assemblies, we can eliminate some of the emotionalism and personal crusading that can make discussions about assemblies so nasty. Recognizing our disagreements, we can then set about the business of developing compromises, new approaches, and whatever else is needed to make the beginning of church school as meaningful as possible for as many as possible.

The first step in developing, maintaining, or cancelling an assembly in the midst of such accepted disagreement is to get very clear about the purpose of the assembly. Indeed, many of the problems with assemblies stem from the fact that people are basing their ideas on assumptions they falsely believe others share. So, the first order of business is to identify and understand those assumptions and to develop a unified purpose from them.

Step #1: What Purpose(s) Do You See in an Opening Assembly?

Pages 81-85 are descriptions of five reasons for having or not having an opening assembly, and some "possibilities to consider" in order to achieve those goals. Begin by reading only the description of each reason. Select the purpose or purposes that most nearly express your view. If you have trouble identifying with any of these, try writing down what you think is a good purpose for an opening assembly. If you are working with a group, share your positions with each other. The point is to be clear and honest about your thinking on opening assemblies.

Step #2: What Purpose Do People at Your Church See in Opening Assemblies?

Now think about the people at your church. What purposes for opening assembly would they cite? On a sheet of paper, write the names of groups or individuals who would support an assembly for each particular purpose. Make qualifying notes where necessary. Try to include all major groups and as many people as possible, but do not get bogged down. This step should take no more than ten minutes. You want an overall picture that is accurate, but not too detailed.

Before moving on, summarize your findings by answering in your own words the question, "What kind of opening assembly, if any, do most people in this church want?"

Step #3: What are the Possibilities for Developing Opening Assemblies That Achieve These Purposes?

Following each "purpose" is a list of "POSSIBILITIES TO CONSIDER" in developing assemblies according to that purpose. Some possibilities suggest ways to discontinue or phase out opening assemblies. Some possibilities suggest ways to avoid dangers in ongoing assemblies. Others describe ways to live with an assembly when you are wishing for something else. Still others outline strategies to capitalize on the strengths of a particular kind of assembly. Read through all the possibilities for each kind of assembly, marking those that you think might be appropriate in your situation.

Step #4: What Can You Do About It?

Using the information you have gathered about what people in your church want and how different kinds of assemblies can be developed, work out (1) a purpose for your opening assembly or the cancellation of your assembly that will be at least partially acceptable to as many people as possible, and (2) a strategy for implementing your chosen direction. The two must go together. For instance, you may realize that the majority of people want an opening ritual. However, you and a significant number of others are interested in developing a closer fellowship in your church. Therefore, you might propose an opening assembly preserving most of the patterns that are already established, and develop a strategy to involve people in sharing their ideas and faith within those rituals.

To complete this step, put into writing your purpose for having or not having an opening assembly. Plan at least one "experiment" in an effort to develop whatever you do to its fullest potential.

NO PURPOSE AT ALL

For some people there is NO purpose to justify an opening assembly. To them it is a hopeless waste of time. They can think of nothing that will salvage it or make it truly meaningful.

Most of these people want the church-school "hour" to be a time for study. They point out that church school is the only time most people give to any form of Christian education. That means that the most regular attender gets only fifty-two hours of education a year (assuming perfect attendance and that there is actually a full hour of education each week)! Given the importance of education and the limited time available for it, these people want to protect the church school from all but education concerns. They want to study during church school, worship during the scheduled congregational worship service, an do business at other times.

They further agree that the worship attempted during an opening assembly is boring and uninspiring. It is led by people who are unable to offer creative leadership to group worship. It is also impossible to provide a complete worship experience of any depth in the time allowed for an opening assembly. A brief scripture reading, a general prayer, and a song are about all there is time for. Such limitations generally result in meaningless worship following prescribed patterns. Because of this, opening assembly can teach children that worship is boring. Given such limitations, some people prefer not to have an opening assembly at all.

POSSIBILITIES TO CONSIDER

★ As the group responsible for the church school, decide to cancel the opening assembly. State clearly the reasons for which you think your church school will be better off without an opening assembly. Submit this decision for approval to the ruling board of your church, if required. Announce the cancellation and reasons for cancellation. Then prepare for the wrath of those who object. At times you will have to be very firm and very patient with a few loud dissenters. Standing firm in the best interest of the church at such times is one of the more difficult parts of church leadership.

★ If there is a wide variety of opinion about the opening assembly, allow each class to decide whether or not it will participate. Non-participating classes begin their studies while others attend the assembly. Children's and youth's classes can often make this decision quietly and stop attending the assembly unnoticed. However, adult classes generally have to be more public about their decision. If everyone is willing to accept the decisions of other classes, this can be the easiest solution to the assembly problem.

★ Because most people of this persuasion want to protect study time, plan your morning schedule around this time. Decide how much time is necessary for study. It may be wise to involve teachers and some students in making this decision. Once you have decided what study time is needed, add the opening assembly to that time before setting the time for church school to begin. Thus, your schedule might be:

9:30-9:45 Opening Assembly
9:45-10:45 Church School Classes
11:00-12:00 Morning Worship

The leaders of the assembly must know that they can no more extend the assembly into class time than teachers could extend class time into the worship service.

★ The freedom that individuals already have to come late in order to miss the opening assembly can be recognized and accepted. You can announce the time for the assembly and the time for classes. People can then be invited to come for one or for both. For this to work, the people who value the assembly and really think that everyone ought to attend have to agree to stop pressuring the later arrivals to come for assembly. It may take some diplomatic reminders to help some people stick by this decision.

★ Replace short weekly assemblies with occasional (perhaps quarterly) church school assemblies that take up the entire church-school time for that day. Appointed planning committees can develop programs that will help students of all ages grow in their faith and worship together. For example, on homecoming, one small church school has a hymn-sing assembly instead of a the regular classes. In addition to singing lots of requests, they choose a few hymns to be explored in depth. The story of the hymn may be told. Its meaning may be explained verbally or in a short skit. If it is based on a specific passage of scripture, that passage is read and compared to the hymn. Some years, the planning committee selects one kind of hymn or hymns from one period of history for special attention. Such an assembly is enjoyed by different people for different reasons. The people who oppose weekly short assemblies often find these longer assemblies very educational and worshipful.

AN OPENING RITUAL

In some churches opening assembly is simply the way church school starts each week. It always has been and probably always will be the way church school starts. This is of no real importance to some people. It is vital to the security and sense of well-being of others.

In some churches, opening assembly is the only totally changeless item on the agenda. As ministers come and go, the worship service reflects their tastes in hymns and messages and style. But in opening assembly the lay people who are born into and die in that church are in control. They sing the songs they cherish, worship in their particular way, and conduct the ongoing business and pastoral concerns of the church in their own style. If the present minister is unpopular, this ritual becomes even more important as an assurance that we, the congregation, will survive even this, and that what is important to us will be upheld in the end. The fact that the assembly tends to be repetitious only makes it more precious in an ever-changing world. Thus opening assembly becomes a celebration of that particular church and its existence across the years.

If opening assembly is this kind of ritual, changing it is challenging much more than "the way we start church school." If, for example, older members of the congregation have been leading people through the same assembly patterns (including memory recitations, their old favorite hymns and even calling on people to lead in prayer without previous warning) that they have used all their lives, and if there is a large number of young families to whom this is meaningless and even embarrassing, there is going to be trouble. The older people will be fighting for the preservation of the church, and if they lose, will in many cases consider themselves "out to pasture" and will give up all leadership to the young people who have "taken over our church."

For most people, the ritual's importance will lie somewhere between these two extremes.

POSSIBILITIES TO CONSIDER

★ If opening assembly is a ritual that is meaningful only to the adults, it may be possible to begin children's and youth classes during the assembly. Often, this happens naturally without announcement. Students hiding out in their classes start helping their teachers get ready for the lesson. Then the teachers begin starting their classes when these students arrive. In this way the adults can enjoy their rituals, while the children and youth are saved from something they dislike. It is possible to encourage this behind the scenes.

★ Try "experiments" when wanting to change a ritual. As the responsible group, declare that you want to try something for a given period (most changes deserve a three-month trial) as an "experiment." Promise that at the end of that period, the idea will be evaluated by all and its future decided. This provides opportunity to live with a possible change for a while and to measure resistance to it. For example, one church school that had been having both opening and closing assemblies, experimented with eliminating the closing assembly in order to give classes more time for their lessons. There was not one complaint, and several appreciative comments. Apparently, closing assembly was not a very important ritual to anyone in that church. That experiment became permanent. On the other hand, one church moved opening assembly from the sanctuary to the fellowship hall in order to make the assembly more informal. The planning committee knew there would be some objections, but thought that during the three months they could revitalize the assembly so much that the objections would quiet down. They were wrong. To the large older adult class, opening assembly *in the sanctuary* was a more important ritual than the planning group thought it was. So at the end of the three months they all returned to the sanctuary. Any further changes they try will be ones that can happen in the sanctuary. The "experiment" enabled them to try something new without a confrontation in which someone came out a loser.

⋆ Protect the ritual, but add another dimension to give it some richness. For example, instead of reading the scripture for the day every Sunday, ask people to take turns leading a devotional (see "POSSIBILITIES" for Celebration of Fellowship). This may deepen the fellowship of the group as people get to know each other better through their turns leading the assembly. Many rituals have the potential for richness and variety within the patterns.

⋆ To keep the ritual from getting stale, assign someone responsibility for the opening assembly. Recruit a person you believe has some talents for, and interest in, this work. Let them know you take their job seriously. Support them as you do teachers, and work with them in planning experiments and evaluating what is going on. (If tradition is that the church-school superintendent leads the assembly, recruit a superintendent who will excel in this task, and relieve him or her of other superintendent tasks as necessary.)

⋆ Sometimes changing a ritual—even one that is meaningless to a large number of people—is not worth the battle. In such cases, do not tamper with the assembly, but insist that it stay within its set time limit. Stay alert to signs of openness to change within the ritual, or signs that the ritual is about to die a natural death. Respond appropriately to each sign.

⋆ Occasionally, opening assembly becomes such a harmful ritual for so many people that someone must intervene. For example, one person gets leadership of the assembly and forces his or her ways and ideas on the others. This situation is especially difficult to handle if the leader is an older person who has contributed much to the church over the years, but who is now out of step with the majority of the congregation. But even in this case, there comes a point at which something must be done. Someone must gather the courage to insist on a change in leadership. While it may take one brave soul to get the process started by talking to the appropriate board, this is a job for the responsible group or the ruling board of the church, rather than an individual acting on personal authority alone. If the board decides to change leadership, it has the authority to enforce its decision. If the board refuses to act, individuals can only endure or withdraw.

⋆ There is one consolation for those who wish they did not have a ritual opening assembly. The assembly can act as a buffer for late arrivals. People may dribble in throughout the assembly. By the time classes begin, all will have arrived, and thus classes will be spared the interruption of late arrivals.

TO BEGIN OUR STUDY WITH WORSHIP

On its shallowest level, beginning church school with worship comes from the belief that every gathering of Christians (and even other groups) should begin with a prayer. This reduces opening prayers to near-superstitious rituals, which offer little meaning but only a format for getting started. In its extreme form, this belief leads to opening prayers at professional football games.

On deeper levels, opening worship springs from the desire to set study in the context of worship. The opening assembly can be an opportunity for all students to prepare themselves for study by consciously coming into God's presence in worship. Though such worship can take place in individual classes, assembling the classes gives the occasion greater dignity and reminds us that all classes are indeed gathered together in God's sight.

POSSIBILITIES TO CONSIDER

⋆ If you are starting church school with worship because "it ought to be done that way," reread the section on "opening ritual" to see if you are not really using worship as a ritual. It can be a temptation to use worship as a way to get everyone started or to quiet them down. This is an abuse of worship. Worship is for the purpose of coming into God's presence. To use it as a means to other ends is to abuse a privilege.

★ Think carefully about the role worship plays in your church school. There are many different ways, all of them good, in which worship can be part of or omitted from church school. For example, some church schools decide to focus on study during the church school hour, encouraging students to worship regularly with the congregation. These schools plan no formal worship services as part of church school. Instead, they train teachers to respond spontaneously to worship moments when they arise during class. Other schools decide that worship is necessary preparation for study, and plan carefully for each class to begin with worship, either in their own room or at some kind of gathering. Still others believe worship and study need to be so integrated that they coordinate the church school and the morning worship service. Each of these approaches has benefits. To get the benefits that are important to you, you must make a conscious decision about the role worship will have in your church school.

★ If your purpose in worship is to prepare for study, plan that worship to be related to the lesson for the morning. For example, one church school, composed mainly of adults studying the International Sunday School Lessons, reads the scripture for the day in the opening assembly. Sometimes the leader reads it. Sometimes it is read in unison. Sometimes it is read responsively. The group also sings a hymn that is related to the lesson. Thus worship truly prepares students for their lesson. The teacher appreciates the fact that all of his students have at least read the day's scripture when class begins.

★ If you want all students to worship together during church school each week, capitalize on this opportunity for people of all ages to learn about worship. Ask classes to prepare all or part of the opening worship. The preschoolers might learn a call to worship to say together one week. Older children might write litanies or prayers for use during this worship. Occasionally, a class might have responsibility for planning and leading the entire assembly. This enables people to learn to worship as they lead in worship. If you do this, coordinate your requests with what classes are studying, so that preparing to lead in assembly does not interrupt a class, but enriches it. For example, if children have prepared a play as part of their study of the defeat of Jericho, they could present the play as part of an opening assembly planned around it the following Sunday.

★ Learn even more about worship by exploring different ways of worshiping during opening assembly. Learn new hymns and their meaning together. Experiment with new ways of praying—for example, the leader pausing to allow others to voice prayers on a given subject. Or try passing the peace as part of your worship. Your minister may want to suggest some things to try in assembly for possible use in congregational worship later.

A CELEBRATION OF THE FELLOWSHIP OF THE FAITHFUL

In some churches the opening assembly is the one regular gathering of members of all ages (Children's Church or nursery may keep young children out of the morning worship service). That makes it an ideal opportunity for knitting people together into an ever-closer community.

In such an assembly at its best the older people enjoy watching the children grow up, and the children have opportunities to meet older adults. Friendships are formed that can carry Christians through the rough times. And real-life Christian heroes and heroines provide models to grow up to.

There are obvious benefits in a fellowshiping assembly, but there are also dangers. It is easy to let such an assembly become a sentimental time to "ooh" and "aah" over each other. Instead of being a "family" that gathers to celebrate and share its faith, it can become an ingrown celebration of self.

POSSIBILITIES TO CONSIDER

★ A "fellowship of the faithful" assembly must be informal. It is much more comfortable sitting in a circle in "the hall" than sitting in rows in the sanctuary. This allows everyone to see everyone else. It allows the leader to sit in the circle as part of the group, rather than stand up front. The youngest children can feel welcome to move around inside the circle a little. No one is overly fearful of taking a turn leading such a gathering of friends.

★ Pass the leadership around. Ask each person (include people of all ages) to take a turn leading the assembly by sharing something of his or her faith and leading the group in prayer. Children can present their favorite Bible stories as plays. Musicians can play a meaningful song (on guitar, piano, or record player) and explain why it is so important to them. Adults can share newspaper articles, poems, favorite scriptures, passages from a book, a picture that tells an important story, and so on. The list is endless. One way to get this started is to have a church school session in which students brainstorm ideas for devotionals, try out a few, and sign up for the day they want to lead the assembly. Most students leave such a session with at least one or two ideas they feel comfortable about developing.

★ Put the focus on individuals. Remember birthdays and other big days simply. Send big cards that include short personal messages from everyone to people who are away from the group.

A QUICK BUSINESS MEETING

One educator recently bemoaned the ending of the opening assembly at her church, because with it she lost the opportunity to explain education plans and policies in an informal setting that allowed questions and answers. She said that people who were at the opening assembly knew and understood (even if they did not always agree with) what was going on in their church.

In small churches in which business is conducted rather informally, the opening assembly can become almost a weekly congregational meeting. Information about sickness, deaths in the family, and other needs for care can be shared, and plans made to respond to them. Details for a fellowship supper, a church retreat, or the revival can be finalized. Potential projects and requests for support can be presented to see how people feel about them before work begins or a decision is made by the appropriate group.

It is easy to see the temptation to carry out more and more church business during church school. One person in a church that had given in to this temptation said, "On Sundays at our church we have one hour of worship and one hour of announcements." Recognizing the power of this temptation and the limited time available for Christian education, many people question giving up any precious education time to conduct business during the opening assembly.

POSSIBILITIES TO CONSIDER

★ Require that any major business items be cleared in advance with whoever coordinates the opening assembly. That way the agenda of the assembly will be within set time limits. If two people have major concerns to air, one can be given time this week, the second promised time next week, and class time for both weeks protected.

★ Avoid duplicating announcements that will be made during worship, unless special discussion is necessary. For example, if World Day of Prayer will be held in a nearby church next week, one announcement is enough. However, if a college choir is singing at that service and your church has promised to host ten choir members, you may want to clear final details during opening assembly as well as announce the event during your worship service. Lists of who is sick, or deaths of people only indirectly related to your church, require only one reading—most likely during the worship hour.

A Closing Word About Opening Assemblies

Opening assemblies at their best are the product of, and reflect, the people who participate in them. The one successful assembly in the group of churches I mentioned earlier is a blend of the celebration of the fellowship of faith and the quick business meeting. As other churches struggled with their assemblies, I occasionally suggested that they try some of the ideas and strategies that had worked so well in the successful assembly. Some of the suggestions proved useful, but many lost their vitality somewhere in the transfer, which brings me to the not-too-startling conclusion that the most effective plans for opening assembly are going to be homegrown. Painful as the struggle is, it is in that struggle that you can create compromises, revitalize dull rituals, and find new ways of doing things that are uniquely appropriate to the people of your church. Do not bemoan the struggle. Use it to develop an ever-stronger church.

Having said that, I close with a list of the only four general statements I know to make about opening assemblies.

No Matter What Its Purpose, Opening Assembly Works Best When . . .

—it starts and ends at a set time. A ruthless leader, who will start on time (even though another car just drove up) and end on time (even if that means interrupting Aunt Martha's sermon), is both a blessing and a necessity.
—it is no longer than ten minutes in length.
—it offers some variety (even within the ritual pattern).
—it is planned with all the people to be included in mind. That means if children are included there must be things meaningful to children and opportunities for them to participate as fully during the opening assembly as the adults do.

Twelve:

Integrating Church School into the Total Life of the Church

A church school often exists almost independently of the rest of the church. It has its own leadership, its own purposes, and sometimes even its own budget. Some people who are deeply involved in the church school are only limitedly involved in the rest of the church's life. Other members, who do not participate in the church school, frequently know nothing about what is going on in the school. All of this leads to the mistaken impression that education is something apart from the main life of the church. Both the church school and the other parts of the church are poorer where this impression is the accepted one.

Christian education is not something that can be separated from the rest of the Christian life or the rest of the church. This is true because . . .

EDUCATION AFFECTS THE WAY PEOPLE WORSHIP. Through education, students learn the history and meaning of our sacraments, our hymns, our creeds, and the other parts of our worship. This knowledge enables students to participate with full understanding in worship. Without this knowledge, worship is a duller and less meaningful experience.

WORSHIP AFFECTS EDUCATION. In worship, students respond to what they explore in study. Worship is an opportunity for students to commit themselves to the message heard and the ideals understood in education. Without this worship opportunity, education is interesting, but does not result in growing faith.

EDUCATION AFFECTS MISSION WORK. Christians do the most effective work when they have a clear understanding of why they are doing this work, based on biblical studies; when they have complete knowledge of the issues involved; and when they have been trained in the necessary skills for the job. For example, the Christian who has studied the biblical texts about our relationship to hungry people and explored some of the complex issues involved in today's hunger crisis, will be both more committed to the church's efforts to minister to the hungry, and better able to contribute effectively to that work.

MISSION WORK AFFECTS EDUCATION. Like worship, mission completes education. In mission, students apply what they have learned. They share the message in words and deeds. Indeed, the power of the message is diluted or lost entirely if it does not lead students to involvement in mission work.

So the truth of the matter is that education is inseparable from all other parts of the Christian life and the rest of the church.

If we accept this truth and begin planning accordingly, we will find that each part of the church's life is a doorway into other parts. For example, a child whose work in church school is incorporated in worship is drawn into participation in the congregation's worship life. In the same way, a service-oriented person can be drawn into study by church-school courses designed to equip people for Christian service. As people are drawn into different parts of the church's life, they grow into a more mature, well-rounded faith. As a result, the church—instead of being a gathering of Christians in which some are students, others are mission-minded, and yet others are worshipers—becomes a community of Christians who work, worship, and study together.

You can see, then, that the case is strong for integrating church school into the total life of the church. There are benefits in it for everyone. And such coordination is quite simple to accomplish! All that is needed is some person or group who is aware of what is going on in different parts of the church's life, and who will point out possibilities for sharing ideas, programs, and work. A number of such possibilities for sharing are described below.

(1) Classes Can Contribute to the Worship Service

Classes, as part of their learning work, often create banners, write prayers and litanies, produce playlets, and so forth, which from time to time could be included in the worship service. For example, a children's class, as part of their study of what a church is, made a large banner. They traced the hands of people in the congregation onto fabric scraps and wrote their names on the "hands." At the center of the banner they printed "You don't join the church, you ARE the church." This was done to stress the idea that the church is people, rather than a club or a building. Their banner hung in the sanctuary for several weeks. On the day they hung it, the minister began the worship service by inviting that class to come up and explain their banner. As the call to worship, he led the congregation in saying in unison the message on the banner.

The seasons of the church year offer special opportunities for classes to contribute to the church's worship. Seasonal banners can be made. During Advent church school, students might study and make ornaments for a Jesse tree or Chrismons tree in the sanctuary. Brief explanations of the ornaments may or may not be included in the worship hour. A class can learn a seasonal song and offer it as an anthem one Sunday morning (this is especially appreciated in churches with no regular choir).

Occasionally, an entire service may be planned and led by one or more classes. The most common example of this is a "Youth Sunday" planned by the youth. But many congregations are now enjoying one or two services a year that are the result of the cooperative study and work of all church-school classes. The celebration of Pentecost, for instance, might be the conclusion of a month's classroom study of that holiday. As part of their study, classes write calls to worship, prayers of confession, creeds, and litanies; choose and learn Pentecost hymns; select appropriate scriptures for the day; and even plan some unusual way to celebrate the day (like sharing birthday cake at the end of the service). The minister may preach as part of such a service, or one class may present a play, a dialogue sermon, or some other way of "preaching the Word" that day.

Though most people would not want a weekly diet of such sharing of church school projects, occasional sharing enriches both worship and the contributing classes.

WARNING: This kind of sharing assumes that people in the congregation are willing to accept all offerings as worthy expressions of worship. The banner described in this section was attractive, but obviously the work of children rather than skilled adults. If a significant number of people are going to object to the inclusion in sanctuary worship of such less-than-perfect expressions, you need to do some homework before subjecting children, youth, or adults to their critical reactions. Perhaps the minister (assuming that he or she is not in the critical group) can preach about what worship expressions are acceptable to God.

(2) The Sermon Can Be Related to a Church School Study

The minister can complement, clarify, or add new dimensions to what is studied in church school. If, for example, the adult class is studying John's gospel, the minister might preach on some of John's other writings and thus enrich the students' understanding of John. Or, if a class studying about the conquering of the Promised Land is raising disturbing, unanswerable questions about God and war, the minister might deal with that issue in a sermon during the course. Most ministers work hard to speak to the current concerns of their congregations, and therefore welcome suggestions or requests about specific sermon needs. When making your request, explain the class situation and the help you need. Your minister may want to see your study materials or visit your class in preparation for a sermon.

(3) Classes Can Be Planned Around a Specific Worship Event

Such classes prepare students to participate in the worship more meaningfully. The most obvious example of this is timing a children's class study of the sacrament of communion to coincide with the church's celebration of the sacrament. After studying the meaning of the sacrament, the children can be involved in setting out the elements for the sacrament, and finally participating in it as their church allows. Integrating the study and the celebration of the sacrament in this way is powerful and has long-lasting effects on a child's participation in the sacrament.

(4) Class Studies Can Grow from or Lead to Mission Work

As people become personally involved in mission work, they often want to study the situation. For example, a young woman who took some old clothes out to a migrant workers ministry center was appalled by the needs she saw. She talked to people working in the center, volunteered some time to help them, and asked her church to help her learn to respond to the needs of migrants. Her church-school class undertook a study of the issue. As a result of this study, she and several others became active in ministry to migrant workers, with the informed support of their classmates.

In a similar situation, a group committed to a certain project might try to involve others in their work through educating them about it. Many denominations produce study materials to draw people into involvement in a variety of mission work. These materials can be used as church-school curriculum. Or, on the local level, the committee planning for the church to sponsor a refugee family may lead classes through a lesson including Bible study, a filmstrip on the organization they will work through, and discussion of the church's involvement in refugee ministry.

In each of these cases church school contributes to, and is enriched by, its integration into the mission work of the church.

(5) Class Studies Can Prepare People to Make Difficult Church Decisions

Churches today are called to take stands on an increasingly wide range of issues, from abortion, criminal justice, children's participation in communion, conscientious objection to the draft, to specific approaches for remedying hunger. None of these are simple issues to respond to. However, church members are often called on to do just that. When a response is sought on a critical issue, many denominations offer materials to help people prepare to make their decisions as wisely as possible. Church-school classes can set aside time to study the materials. In so doing, they inform students of the issues that are facing the Christian church today, and offer them opportunities to grow as they apply their faith to these issues.

How Can We Do These Things?

As I said at the beginning of the list of ways to integrate church school into the total life of the church, none of the items is particularly sophisticated or complex. All that is required is a person or group who is aware of what is happening in all parts of the church's life, and is aware of some of the ways the church school can share with them. The minister can often be this person. Since ministers are in charge of the worship service, they often take the lead in integrating church school and worship. They can work with a class as it plans a contribution to or participation in a worship service.

But it is also important that whatever group is responsible for the overall church-school program be involved in attempts to integrate the church school into other parts of the church. It is important because unless everyone is clear about what is being done and why it is being done, there is going to be trouble. Teachers will accuse mission committees of stealing their time. Worshipers will claim that the church school is trying to take over the morning worship hour. If some group is overseeing coordination efforts, they can interpret those efforts publicly in advance, and thus avoid the majority of the conflicts. In time, that committee will also become aware of special needs and concerns that affect coordination. For example, they may discover a class that is unanimous in its wish not to be diverted from studying their particular lesson series in their particular way. They may also identify a class anxious to get involved in a specific part of the church's life. That kind of knowledge is extremely helpful.

The responsible committee can contribute further to this effort by doing long-range planning. Such planning enables the church school to relate to a variety of parts of the church each year, instead of responding to possibilities only as they arise. Thus, one year the committee may plan for all classes to study the denomination's world mission emphasis materials during February, for the youth class to plan a Youth Sunday at the conclusion of their summer study of worship, and can be alert for opportunities for other classes to contribute to worship. Further requests would be considered in relationship to these commitments and the classes' other study plans.

Conscious efforts to integrate the church school into the life of the church reap great rewards—especially in small churches. Because we are small, we need nearly everyone's participation in almost all areas of our church life. This need becomes an asset because, as we all worship, work, and study together, we become more aware of ourselves as a church, a community of God's people; and we recognize the richness and potential of that community as a whole.

Assignment

Answer the following questions:

(1) Is your church school a part of the church's life that is related to all other parts?

(2) Below is a list of ways the church school can be integrated into the life of your church. Place a check in front of each way in which your church school is currently related to other parts of the church's life. Place a check after each way you want to try during the coming year (try only one or two new ideas each year).

Have tried		Want to try
______	Classes contribute to the worship service	______
______	Sermon related to church-school studies	______
______	Classes planned around a specific worship event	______
______	Classes related to the church's mission	______
______	Classes preparing people for church decision-making	______

(3) Make the plans necessary to further integrate the church school into the life of your church, using the methods selected in number 2 above.

Part Three:
Christian Education Is More Than Church School

In some discussions one can get the idea that "Christian education" and "church school" are interchangeable terms. If this were true, churches with well-functioning church schools could consider their education ministry complete. Similarly, a church serious about providing Christian education could begin its work by asking "How can we start a church school?" In another church, the members, who might feel the need for better opportunities for Christian education, could try to fill that need by asking "What can we do to improve our church school?"

But "Christian education" and "church school" are NOT interchangeable terms. Christian education describes *all* our efforts to enable people to grow in their faith. Church school is only one of the many ways we provide opportunities for this growth. As an organization, the church school has no scriptural base (Christian education does). Indeed, the church school is only two hundred years old. That means the church existed and provided opportunities for Christian growth for nearly eighteen hundred years without any Sunday church schools.

Therefore, the church's mission is, not to build church schools, but to provide members opportunities for Christian education. The opening question for a church concerned about the Christian growth of its members is not "How can we provide a church school?" but "What do our members need now to keep growing in their faith?" In the smallest of churches we can answer that question on an individual basis.

The fourteen-year-old musician may grow most by taking on music leadership for the summer (giving the usual leader a deserved vacation). As music leader, the teenager could work with the minister to choose hymns that fit the scripture and sermon each week, and play for the worship services. In that work she or he would grow in the understanding of and appreciation for the music of the church.

Two or three active ten-year-olds might be ready to grow by serving. The "responsible group" could set them up with a service project. In that project they would learn about a very specific mission need and grow in their sense of being a contributing part of the church.

Small groups of adults with special concerns can be invited to short-term week-night courses exploring that concern.

If such plans are being made for the growth of individuals, a church may have no need at all for a church school. Such a church has no need to apologize to itself or anyone else about the fact that it maintains no church school, because it is involved in the ministry of Christian education. Even if it does operate a church school, a church that takes Christian education seriously will want to ask regularly whether there are needs for education to which the church school is not responding.

In either case, there are many possibilities for doing good Christian education beyond the church school. Some of the possibilities simply require that you recognize the educational potential in a current program and develop it. Other possibilities require setting up new programs or planning special events. The remainder of this chapter is a list of descriptions of opportunities for Christian education that can be implemented in most small churches.

(1) Youth Fellowship

Many churches that attempt no other Christian education beyond the church school, make some attempt to sponsor a youth fellowship. Such fellowships often attract more young people than any other part of the church, including worship.

The informal atmosphere of a fellowship provides opportunities for significant education of a very particular sort. Formal "programs" or "lessons" that include laborious study and feel like school are OUT in successful fellowships. Exploring teen issues, using simulation games, dramatics, and values exercises, is IN. Projects are even more IN. Fellowship can be a time for learning by doing, a chance to try out "being the church." It is a time to visit different kinds of churches, sponsor hunger hikes, tour the denominations' headquarters on a trip that combines learning and recreation, meet the people who serve in the local Salvation Army, "canvass" each other about their financial responsibility to the church, and even visit a foreign mission field.

Leading such a fellowship, even a small one, is challenging, fun, and exhausting. The job requires more than the work of one or two advisors. The advisors need the active support of the "responsible group." For starters, they need the same care and feeding that every teacher gets. They especially need a group that keeps informed of their plans, even contributes to shaping those plans, and makes extra help available when needed. Under this kind of shared leadership, a fellowship can be the most educational experience a teen-ager has in the church.

(2) After-School Church Clubs

On Sunday morning the average church-school class has thirty minutes or less of pure study time. If children and youth are brought to the church after school one afternoon each week, one-and-a-half to two hours are available.

The time may be divided between some or all of the following: Bible study, recreation, group singing or children's choir rehearsal, worship, and education and service projects. This means there is time for learning activities that simply is not available on Sunday mornings. Field trips, the production of whole plays, cantata rehearsals, messy or complex art activities, movies, simulation games, and more can fit into the schedule of an afternoon. The sum of these experiences can enable participants to keep growing and learning in ways they enjoy.

Some denominations and publishers offer printed resources for after-school church clubs. Churches that cannot find one of these programs that meets their standards may use a church-school curriculum or create their own plans using the wealth of resources available today.

With the rising popularity of camping, skiing, mountain cabins, and beach cottages many churches that can no longer gather a crowd for Sunday morning classes find after-school church clubs an excellent replacement. Other churches plan for the clubs to supplement what is offered in the church school.

(3) Vacation Bible School

This traditional education effort is so well known that it hardly needs mentioning. However, because it is a tradition, it often is rerun annually without much development of its full potential. We simply order the curriculum we have always ordered, divide into the traditional classes, sing the same Bible school songs, play the same games, and snack on the traditional juice and cookies. Since Bible school may be our most concentrated, or even our only, contact with some children, the opportunity deserves careful consideration.

Instead of duplicating church school on a grander scale, many small churches are attempting to offer opportunities in Bible school that are beyond the scope of church school or anything else offered by the church. For example, several small churches have joined forces to plan for a week-long Bible Day Camp. Over one hundred children and youth turn out annually for study, recreation, and special projects at a nearby camp (which offers the added drawing card of a swimming pool). They further capitalize on the opportunity each year by choosing a special project or focus. For instance, because none of the churches have children's choirs, they have sometimes devoted the week to preparing a children's musical about a Bible story. When they do this, they study the story, learn songs for the musical, and make costumes and props. These sorts of ventures take full advantage of the opportunity offered by Bible school.

(4) Family-Night Suppers

Churches that enjoy quarterly, monthly, or just occasional family-night suppers have a natural opportunity to do "family" or "intergenerational" learning. After the dishes are cleared away, people of all ages are usually quite willing to spend some time together in some not-too-academic learning. There are several books (available in most religious bookstores) that include directions for intergenerational events, from Advent gift-making workshops to family living exercises. Or you may view and discuss a short film rented or borrowed from a church film library. Or you can design a program to meet a specific need. One small Presbyterian church, for example, responded to heated discussions and deep concerns about children's participating in the Lord's Supper with a family-night program in which families could explore the meaning of the sacrament together.

(5) Retreats

We generally think of a retreat as something for energetic teen-agers. However, a retreat is a chance to get away or be apart. People of all ages relish such chances. Many churches, recognizing that fact, are offering a variety of retreats as opportunities for Christian growth. Instead of weekly church school, one church plans a monthly, in-church, Friday supper through Saturday afternoon retreat, for children grades two through eight. They claim that they can offer better leadership and more interesting learning experiences for the children in this way than they could on Sunday mornings. In other churches, the officers go on an annual retreat for training and preparation for their year's work. Still other churches look forward to a weekend all-church retreat at a nearby church camp. These retreats include educational programs and themes, but the fellowship shared often teaches more about what a Christian community is called to be than any book lesson ever could.

(6) Short-Term Week-Night Courses

Many adults who are either looking for more than they are getting in church school, or unwilling to commit themselves to regular Sunday morning class attendance, enjoy occasional short-term week-night courses. Such courses provide opportunities to explore church concerns such as the charismatic movement, do in-depth studies of particularly difficult parts of scripture such as Revelation, or follow a seasonal emphasis. Week nights offer more informal and open-ended sessions than Sunday classes, with their rigid schedules, allow. Week-night classes may also offer the opportunity for the minister, who cannot teach on Sundays, to teach classes.

Few churches offer week-night courses as a regular ministry. Instead, they may offer one at a given time each year. The season of Lent is one time many Christians undertake such additional study as part of their Lenten discipline or preparation for Easter. The six weeks of Lent make for a course of comfortable length. Other churches prefer to schedule such courses as the need arises.

(7) Worship Preparation Study Groups

Some ministers have begun inviting members of their congregations to meet with them to study in preparation for the following Sunday's worship. Meeting early in the week, the group studies the scriptures for the worship, and discusses their meaning for their church. They may even discuss hymns that would be appropriate and ways the message of the scriptures could influence prayers of confession, intercession, and praise. All of this serves a double purpose. It helps the minister prepare to lead in worship, and it helps others prepare to worship more fully.

(8) Annual Events

Every church has a collection of traditions and annual events that are simply part of "the way we do things." The collection varies from church to church—and may include such dissimilar things as the church school picnic in June, the children's Christmas pageant the Sunday night before Christmas, Easter sunrise service followed by breakfast cooked by the men, Rally Day the second Sunday in September, a Chrismons tree, a chicken-wire cross filled with flowers on Easter—and the list goes on. These are as much the rituals of the church as the way you observe the sacraments. Because of that, they are also opportunities for powerful teaching. For example, the children could each be assigned their lines in a published pageant, told to memorize them, run through a chaotic rehearsal or two, and applauded. Or, the children could be gathered to explore the Christmas story and decide how they want to present it. Older children could write lines, if necessary. The group could choose any music they want, paint scenery, make slides, plan dances, and select other ways of sharing their message. The resulting program may look a lot like the preplanned pageant, or it may not be as good; but the children will have learned much more by preparing it themselves. There are similar opportunities for education in each of the other annual events at your church. It is your task to identify the opportunities and develop them. You will discover that the events grow in their meaning as rituals as a result of your work.

(9) Mission Projects

The main purpose of mission projects is, of course, to help other people. However, such projects also offer the helpers opportunities for learning. The most striking example in my experience has been a presbytery-sponsored project of building a public health center in Zaïre. Long-range fund raising was based on asking each person in the presbytery's churches to contribute two cents per meal. Stickers were provided for labeling penny jars for use on family tables. Filmstrips about the area to be served and the services to be offered by the proposed center were circulated. As people got involved in the project they became knowledgeable about the economic realities that affect daily life in Zaïre, public health programs in developing nations, and the work of the native Christian church in Zaïre. They became personally involved in the lives of the missionaries and Zarois Christians as letters were exchanged about progress on the project. No church school lesson or "program" could have taught so many people so much about a distant part of God's family. At the same time, many mission projects do not accomplish this kind of education. This one was educational because the planners planned for it to be. Their fund-raising strategy was designed to make a big impact on individuals. They presented the project with pictures of the people involved and clear descriptions of what they were up against and what they hoped to do about it. You can do the same kind of planning in order that mission projects sponsored by your church be educational for the sponsors, as well as helpful to those for whom they are intended.

(10) The Sacraments

The sacraments, because they express in action the central beliefs of our faith, are powerful teachers. Their power can be maximized if you plan accordingly.

Baptism, whether of an infant, a young person, or an adult, marks an entry into the community of faith. Confessions of faith and promises are made. People generally take these confessions and promises very seriously. Their "seriousness" makes them very open to instruction about the meaning of the sacrament and the ways in which they can carry out their vows. Just as many churches require that couples counsel with the minister about Christian marriage before the wedding ceremony, churches need to require parents or candidates for baptism to discuss the sacrament at some depth with the minister and/or several members of the ruling board. Such instruction will not only increase persons' understanding of the sacrament, but can lead them to grow through the experience of the sacrament into a fuller Christian life. (Ministers in large churches would have difficulty finding time for this kind of Christian education. Again, in small churches, we are lucky.)

An alert minister can make the celebration of a baptism educational for the whole church. Children can be invited to stand up front where they can see. In introducing the sacrament, the minister can comment briefly on some aspect of it that is particularly meaningful in this situation. Thus, with every baptism, the congregation grows in its understanding of the sacrament.

A minister can use many of the same tactics to teach members of the congregation more about the meaning of communion each time it is observed. In addition, individuals can be invited to take a turn preparing the bread and drink for the sacrament. For families with children this can lead to important discussion about the meaning of the elements as the bread is baked and the drink poured. In these sharing times, children begin to sense the value their parents place on both the sacrament and the faith it represents. In the same way, people of all ages can grow in their understanding of and appreciation for communion if they are invited to share in taking it around to shut-in members of the church.

The sacraments teach. With some conscious efforts on our part they can teach even more.

(11) Committee Meetings

Yes, even committee meetings offer opportunities for and demands for Christian education. Unfortunately, these are usually ignored. Instead, members deal as concisely as possible with the items on their agenda and hope to get home early. This is unfortunate, because such committees never get any new ideas about their work or ways to carry it on. The church is producing an overwhelming amount of resources on nearly every part of its life and work. Committee members need to explore and evaluate the ideas in some of the resources related to their work. When they do not, their work becomes pretty much a matter of doing again what has been done before, for lack of any better ideas.

What a difference it would make if committees set aside time to study the scriptures related to their work, to learn about new programs and ideas being pursued in their area of responsibility, or to consciously study all sides of an issue before a decision was made! It can be done. Some committees do set aside time at each meeting for their own continuing education. In that time, a Christian education committee might study Old Testament passages about child rearing at one meeting, hear and discuss a brief book report on a new book about some aspect of Christian education during the next meeting, read a denominational position paper on the church's responsibility to prepare young people for confirmation at another meeting, and so on. The results of their study will be apparent in the work the committee does. Furthermore, after a term on such a committee, a person not only would have done his or her share of the work, but also would have gained a fuller picture of the education ministry and its possibilities. For example, I recently talked with a stranger on a plane. This young man enthusiastically described his work as a member of the ruling board of his church of two hundred members. He said that he had been surprised by some of the things that group had struggled with and the ways they struggled. He concluded by saying, "Since I have been serving on the board, I have learned more about the church and grown more in my understanding of what it means to be a Christian than I have in my whole life." Both the individual and the church benefit from this kind of learning through serving on a working group or committee.

(12) Men's and Women's Groups

Last, but most definitely not least, there are education opportunities of many kinds in the men's and women's groups in your church. Often meetings of these groups include programs and Bible studies whose purpose is education. Many people who will never be coaxed into the church school participate in these programs and studies regularly. Thus it behooves the church to be sure these educational efforts are top quality. The group responsible for Christian education may or may not have authority to direct the educational work of these groups. Such groups often have their own printed curriculum or series of preplanned programs. Though these vary in quality, they usually have to be accepted. But, given those limitations, there are ways to influence the education done in these groups. Women's organizations are often broken down into smaller units to meet in homes for study and fellowship. Even a small church will often have two or more of these groups. The minister can improve the quality in all of them at once by meeting with the study leaders to prepare the lesson for each month. Such an effort is both appreciated and effective.

As you can see, the list of ways small churches can provide members opportunities for Christian education is long and varied. The list in this chapter is by no means exhaustive. Indeed, the list may have called to mind opportunities that are unique to your church. That is grand. Your job is NOT to produce the "proper Christian education ministry" following directions in any manual, or duplicating what works somewhere else. Instead your job is to create opportunities for the particular people in your particular church to grow in their faith in ways that are appropriate for them.

Assignment

Below is a list of all the opportunities for Christian education beyond the church school that are included in this chapter.

(1) Read through the list, checking in the first column those items that are being developed to their educational potential in your church.

(2) There is space left for you to add to the list other educational efforts being made by your church. Take time to identify more than the obvious ones.

(3) Go back through your list, and discuss ways you could develop each item in your church. Finally, check one or two items that you want to consciously develop during the coming year (next year you may want to select some others to work on).

(4) Make the necessary plans to begin developing the educational potential of the selected items. For example, if you want to develop the educational potential of family-night suppers, you may want to assign someone the job of locating a book of intergenerational programs, decide that you will take responsibility for planning two educational suppers during the coming year, and set aside time on your agenda to do this planning.

We are doing		Let's develop further
______	youth fellowship	______
______	after-school church clubs	______
______	vacation Bible school	______
______	family-night suppers	______
______	retreats	______
______	short-term week-night classes	______
______	worship preparation study groups	______
______	annual events	______
______	mission projects	______
______	sacraments	______
______	committee meetings	______
______	men's and women's groups	______
______		______
______		______
______		______
______		______
______		______

Epilogue

Throughout this book I have urged you not to be enslaved by anyone else's idea of how Christian education ought to be done in a church. The same goes for the ideas in these chapters. They are not blueprints for the education ministry that your church ought to be providing. In fact, if a small church tried to implement every idea in these chapters, it would exhaust its minister and drive its members crazy. The point is not to do everything, but to select those forms of Christian education that fit your church, and to do them very well. In doing this, I expect you will find yourselves capable of providing your members with opportunities to grow in their faith that will prove interesting, exciting, and more effective than you ever dreamed possible.